Thinking About
Thinking With NLP

by
Joseph Yeager, Ph.D.

Meta Publications
P.O. Box 565
Cupertino, California 95014

Library of Congress Card Number 85–063154
I.S.B.N. 0–916990–16–8

FOREWORD

Neuro-Linguistic Programming is now a decade old and the extent of its impact is still expanding every year. It is by now obvious that NLP is not merely a "ripple in the new wave of pop psychology" but rather an entire system of knowledge for more effectively managing all areas of human endeavor. Grinder and Bandler did not merely invent new procedures for psychotherapists as one might invent a new surgical procedure. They redefined the goals and presuppositions of the field of behavioral change in general. This has been the most important contribution of NLP.

There have now been many books written about NLP, but very few of them address the applications and contributions of NLP on this most important macro level. It is Joe Yeager's ability to grasp, integrate and state the fundamental principles of NLP in a succinct and entertaining way that makes this book so special. This is a book of new ideas, not simply a rehash of existing NLP techniques stated in different jargon.

For example, a lot of lip service has been given to the notion that NLP has a lot to offer to the business world. Up until the time I met Joe, however, it seemed that most of the applications of NLP in the areas of business and management centered around incorporating this or that NLP technique into some other sales or management model as an enhancement. Joe on the other hand uses the principles, modeling techniques, skills, and most importantly the attitude of NLP to approach the whole field of business management and, more generally, people management. This creates an entire change in perspective and orientation toward the goals and procedures of effective management that approaches the paradigm shift in physics caused by Einstein's theory of relativity.

Rather than simply talk about how eye movements or rapport may be used as an additional skill in sales or management, Joe uses the most fundamental principles of NLP to refine and challenge the basic presuppositions of organization and management. Joe's comprehensive approach opens the doorway to a whole new level of development and application of NLP. The result extends far beyond any attempt that has been made to adapt some therapeutic technique to a business context. I believe that it is only through Joe's comprehensive approach that the full power of NLP can be realized in the business community.

Even more impressive is that Joe has been able to generate and extend these insights to include the entire scope of the behavioral sciences.

As a developer, author and trainer in the field of NLP it is a rare treat to be in the position where someone else can put my own intuitions so elegantly into words.

Robert Dilts
Scotts Valley, Ca.

ACKNOWLEDGMENT

I acknowledge *everybody!!* When all my family, friends, teachers and colleagues see me after reading this and I smile at them, they will know I am acknowledging them and thanking them again. This is the best way I know to cover all the bases in an acknowledgement.

The content of the book came from the work being done at the Eastern NLP Institute so it seems logical to thank the Institute as well. However, since I am one of the bosses at the Institute, along with Linda Sommer, that amounts to thanking myself, too. O.K., me, you're welcome.

Richard Bandler might just as well have written this book. All of the essential ideas were originally his. I was just lucky enough to put them in my words and persuade him to publish the results. He continues to produce the creative developments that will lead the field into the next century. I thank him lots and lots. His genius and friendship have given me the substance of my work for most of the last decade. Given the opportunity, he will also eliminate seriousness as an international problem.

Robert Dilts and I have done enough brainstorming and laughing together to last a lifetime and I expect to repeat that experience with him *ad infinitum* over the coming years. You will find echos of his influence throughout the book. As you read those ideas, you might thank him as much as I do. His gentleness and caring are well known. I hope some of it has rubbed off on me and that it shows.

Linda Sommer, who is president of the Eastern NLP Institute, is mentioned frequently for good reason. Her brainpower is on a par with Richard and Robert. It would be hard to find a quicker mind anywhere. Her influence and ideas are everywhere in the book. And she knows how to throw a good party.

As Robert mentioned recently, the center of gravity of NLP is located in the company of people who work directly with Richard. It is a pleasure to be part of that very productive group of people which includes Chris Hall, Michael Vandiver, Steven Drozdeck, Will MacDonald, Max Steinbach, Ed and Maryann Reese, Robert Dilts, Todd Epstein, The Society of Neuro-Linguistic Programming and a cast of thousands too numerous to mention or to invite to Linda's parties.

Peggy Dean deserves special mention. She is an accomplished executive and, happily, is on the staff of the Institute. She steered the events that were necessary to bring the manuscript into being. Without her discipline and ability, lots of things would have taken much longer. She is an effective antidote to my slothful nature and poorish memory.

If events continue to evolve as they have, there will be an entire series of books, programs and trainings emerging from this cluster of people. Their ideas and productivity are impressive by any standard. Then they will all have the happy tasks of thanking one another and having to figure out their own way of covering all the bases in an acknowledgment. After all, they can't thank *everybody*, as I have . . . or can they?

Joseph C. Yeager, Ph.D.
Eastern NLP Institute, P.O. Box 697, Newtown, PA 18940

ON IMAGINATION, SCIENCE, POWER AND TRANSCENDENT GOALS

An age-old dream of psychology has arrived. The discovery of Neuro Linguistic Programming (NLP) puts behavioral science on a par with other "hard" sciences. At the turn of the century, psychologists were very much preoccupied with pretentiously apeing the hard science of physics in an attempt to deal with the slippery phenomena of human behavior. However, the status of psychology didn't ascend much beyond the level of philosophy and theology in the opinion of many observers.

It is a curious thing to look backward and find that so many people *almost* discovered NLP. Certainly the ancient Greeks could have discovered NLP because the science requires no hardware. Aristotle probably came close.

But one of my favorite "near misses" is that of Sir Francis Galton, the British scientist who studied mental imagery. He used a type of analysis on his data that missed the point entirely. Had he asked "How do these individuals differ?" he would have done much better than he did by asking "How do people behave *on the average?*" He unknowingly sacrificed the mechanisms of individual thinking for generalities. In fact it would have been smart if he had asked both questions.

At the very different levels of the consumer's day-to-day experience versus the scientific explorer's lofty probing of the unknown, NLP is equally effective and productive. Some argue that NLP is interdisciplinary. That is a nice enough compliment about it's broad scope and value. More to the point, NLP is *meta* disciplinary. NLP approaches and possibly even succeeds at identifying the perpetual search for "first principles" in human events.

Richard Bandler has even gone to the trouble to demonstrate, for example, that mathematics is a behavioral science. That may sound odd, but NLP transcends the abstract symbols of math to arrive at the thinking and symbolic processes of mind. In part at least, NLP is the science of thinking about thinking . . . hence, the title of this book.

In that sense, all fields are subordinate to psychology, since all other fields spring from the mind. Our mind "constructs" reality. That is, we have to *learn* reality since we are not given a fixed definition via "instinct." Since mental constructions are relative, so is the notion of first principles—the first principle might well be that there are no first principles.

Even though it may take a generation for the "publication lag" to spread the word of NLP's breakthrough status, many of the age old questions of human behavior now have evolved from the realm of superstition, folklore, theory, theology and common sense to the levels of technology, engineering and science.

NLP may eventually be ranked by science as one of the more spectacular discoveries of our age. If NLP were measured by results alone, it certainly has outperformed any of it's comparable predecessors. The rate of change in human behavior which NLP routinely produces far outstrips other dominant schools of psychology. For any practitioner in the realm of human nature, the field has become a breakthrough in predictable results. Human behavior isn't quite so quicksilvery as before.

I am reminded that Buckminster Fuller once wrote a book titled *Operating Manual for Spaceship Earth.* In a comparable sense, the work of Richard Bandler, et. al. has given us the first draft of what I would like to call *The Operating Manual for*

Human Nature. Richard has a book in press called *Using Your Brain For A Change.* The "manual" has a complex coding structure that gives us the promise of what linguists call "compositionality." That is, language mechanisms in the brain are arranged by nature so that a relatively few "rules" can be combined in essentially infinite ways. This plastic nature of our innate thinking mechanisms is paralleled in the coding structure of NLP. This efficient and effective structure gives NLP a leg up on the intellectual competition.

Of course, this raises the inevitable issue of the uses of such a powerful technology. Ethical issues abound. But those issues are not new. Those concerned with dominating their fellow humans with it will do so. Those concerned with improving the lot of their fellow humans will do so. In sum, NLP will have changed nothing in the overall equation of human motives. However, on at least one level of understanding, it will increase the contrast between dominance and imagination and force us to make clear choices.

One of the definitions of NLP that bears study is this assertion: NLP is the science of "choice." Deterministic thinking is part and parcel of science. Yet one of our curious goals is to be able to transcend determinism for the values of free will. One of the ways I model this is found in a chapter where I describe the "decision tree model" I use to represent choices available to the person at any given moment in time. Most choices are finite options in common experience. Even the notion of people "deciding" at identifiable "choice points" is itself a construction that is not universally held as "the way reality is."

Many oriental schools of thought don't structure their reality in terms of discrete choices but rather think of thinking as continuous and fluid with little or no model of individual choice. In other words, *choice* is a convention of thinking, not a given of human nature. NLP hasn't brought this classic dispute over free will to closure. But it has evolved the tools of the argument to the point that we have greater "requisite variety" when we think about those issues. That may lead us somewhere surprising.

Certainly, we are about to reach the stars if we don't reach for the Armageddon button first. If we are to reach the stars successfully, we are going to have to figure out how to transcend our roots of dominance behavior. We are facing the prospect of genetic engineering and other developments that will have powerful influence upon our nature and our future as a species.

It also comes to mind that most of the "decisions" that are made by those in control of the superpower nations are made essentially the same way as the average spouse or young child on a playground picks a fight. The fact that a minor kinesthetic event in the neurology of a senior military or government official could cause him to push the button that would send us all into oblivion is, to me, the ultimate in curious circumstances.

I also find Alice in Wonderland making a lot more sense as I get more experience. As a result, my thinking has paid a great deal of attention to the issues of power compared to other motives such as achievement, sex, creativity and affiliation . . . not that I wanted to, but because it has proven to be necessary. It is my subjective view of where the action is in many ways. That area of attention to power is pervasive in my thinking of what NLP is and what it means to myself and to others.

In a closely related line of inquiry, Jay Haley has written some very valuable things about the connection of subjective experience to power-related phenomena. When teaching, I classify mammals arbitrarily into three types: solitary animals such as tigers; herd animals such as cattle; hierarchical animals such as baboons and humans. It is pretty obvious to even the most casual observer, that our hierarchical nature is our most pervasive characteristic and the framework or context of most of our subjective experience.

In sum, NLP is a science and technology that is delivered by the vehicle of the values of its practitioners. One of our first principles as explorers in this new field is to follow such a phenomenon wherever it leads. But the corollary of that principle for me is to be sure of my values so that I know what I want it to do for others when we arrive at milestone choices.

CONTENTS

CHAPTER ONE

THINKING ABOUT THINKING WITH NLP

There are three lines of thought, I've discovered, when talking to behavioral scientists about Neuro Linguistic Programming (NLP). One is the group that's learned all it wants to learn and has decided that no amount of argument or reasoning is going to change its mind about using NLP. The second group consists of those who use NLP and they are, for better or worse, the True Believers. These people can be evangelistic. I have seen others evade true believers and they resemble Joe Frazier's moves to avoid Ali. I may be one of these evangelists. After all, I can cure a phobia or some other bad habit in five minutes with NLP and no other psychology can claim that result.

But the third group is the largest, ranging from those who have never even read an article about NLP (but are now) to those who have been seduced by the payoffs of the new technology even if they haven't yet learned it themselves as well as they'd like. This group is growing in size.

Some people think the main reasons for using NLP is to be in control of a dialog or to speed up the time it takes to get a change in behavior such as changing a decision, an opinion, a mood, a habit or compulsion, etc. To those ends the key reason is to get *more* of the results you want.

This is true but not all of the truth. To my way of thinking, NLP is the most efficient and effective means of enhancing human behavior that exists. As the Research Institute for the Executive has noted, "It is the most powerful means for change in existence." I believe it. And I hold certificates in other competing systems of behavioral science such as Biofeedback, Hypnosis, Rational Emotive Therapy, Family Systems Therapy, and more.

As I sit at my word processor, I make inevitable comparisons to my old typewriter and the enormous gains in effectiveness and productivity that arise from my new technical marvel on the microchip. The gains in my work in therapy, consulting and management that NLP has provided over other modes of behavioral science are by comparison a quantum leap beyond even the amazing gains I obtained with the word processor over my typewriter.

Effectiveness and productivity are words not often found in combination with human events. Most people associate them with factories and machinery. But, I do literally mean that effectiveness and productivity happen even in the context of therapy, or education, or consulting, or management, or law or . . . So there!

My productivity has improved in measurable ways. I can get to the heart of a consulting interview in minutes instead of hours. I can reduce the average number of therapy interviews by at least fifty percent, and often by over seventy-five percent. That is a lot of saved money for my clients, but it does present the opposing problem of meaning that I have to be more active in getting referrals since turnover in clients is rather rapid. Rarely does an individual client need more than a half-dozen sessions.

It is now difficult for a therapist to justify seeing a client for years when in a matter of a few sessions the majority of presenting problems are resolved. My ability to precisely select the effective procedure also means that the result I get with a client is virtually 100% predictable. Ask your average therapist if they know what procedure they are going to use in a given situation and what the specific outcome will be. Most will hedge and be very general and wish NLP would go away at that point.

In other words, quality is also improved for the receiver of my services in addition to it happening a lot faster. I would not use a discovery like NLP if it negatively affected the quality of what I do.

Recently I had a conversation with Dr. Norman Stander, and industrial psychologist of considerable competence in the area of management, who probably holds some sort of record for erudition in his field. We talked about the issues surrounding NLP because he was curious about the newest technology I had chosen to use in my unusual (or maverick, if you like) combination of career interests. He wanted to know some things about it: why I had trained in it, what I thought of it now that I was certified in it, how it compared to other systems, and so on.

I answered his questions with a bit of anticipation about a key issue I thought he would bring up since he is the essense of ethics and rectitude. I knew what he would ask before he said it. "Is this technology manipulative? You know, it sounds like it gives you an awful lot of control over the other person . . ." "No," I replied, "but I know what you mean." I get the question all the time. It's a question born in the post-Freudian era of folks being suspicious that the analyst had some secrets from them as he or she would comment authoritatively, "Aha!" So you *did* argue with your mother."

Feeling criticized, bushwhacked, and nauseated all at the same time was a typical response to feeling that the analyst had laid a trap and maneuvered you into it. It is surprising how many people have an aversion to psychologists of any kind as a result of that stereotype. The only problem I have with this manipulation phobia that runs rampant through our society is this: it implies that if you know what you are doing, you are being manipulative.

Try that logic the next time you talk to your Financial counselor or your physician or your accountant. If they didn't know exactly how to cause the results you'd want, you'd scream to high heaven . . . and maybe even to Ralph Nader. It is no different when you are a "Nelper" (as we affectionately call ourselves). We simply know what we are doing a whole lot better than do a lot of other applied parts of the psychological community. We know how to fix depressions, anxiety attacks, stress syndromes, learning disorders and more in as little as one session.

If we know how to cause results, what is wrong about that? The real issue is trust and either you trust the practitioner to help you, or you don't. And that's that.

Everyone has seen the inviting ads in popular magazines offering things like instant memory or the key to magical mental skills. Maybe they work, maybe they don't. But the fact is that any human thought or feeling event that goes on in a person can be captured with "Nelping" methods. The lucky few who have spontaneously learned how to have amazing mental skills can serve as specific models and their mental skills can be duplicated for you and me to use with the same results they get.

This is the result of "Nelpers" knowing exactly how to *change* your thinking habits, not just *talk about* them.

No doubt, those with negative attitudes toward NLP share parallel feelings with those typists who have been required to learn a lot about the more productive word processor in order to keep up. It is complicated to learn in some ways, but the results are more than worth the effort in payoff later. Both of these resisters of change may feel that innovation is not to be taken seriously—not for *experienced* people anyway. Some seem to feel that NLP technology has infringed on a territory that is the last haven of the "humanist" who insists on playing everything by ear.

This attitude when translated into practical terms means

that the fuzzy and intentionally planless psychologist thinks he or she has the right to indulge personal feelings and attitudes at the expense of the client. No doubt they view a technological approach the end of "humanness" in applied psychology and see all of us being made into obedient ciphers.

It goes to show they don't think much of their clients' ability to learn and to profit from improved situations . . . unless, of course, the friendly, humanistic psychologist is around to guide them at $? per hour.

NLP is no more than the learning tool of its time. Nelping is, quite simply, the most amazing thing that has happened to behavioral science in years—maybe even generations. And most of the professionals in this country don't know about it. They have no idea that one of the greatest things that could ever come into their lives has already arrived.

Maybe the Vikings had the same problem in that they didn't know they had discovered the New World. Well, at least it gave the Indians another thousand years to enjoy themselves before the rest of us showed up.

As for those who do realize it, I've yet to speak to a professional who uses NLP who isn't absolutely ecstatic about it.

There's a lot of confusion over NLP. The technology has snowballed so quickly that the term NLP and the prospect of learning it is likely to make some prospective users break out in hives. But, as the demon of learning it has raised its head, so have the exorcists to deal with it. There are over two dozen books in the field to help you learn NLP, and there are several Institutes with monthly sessions and year-long training programs leading to Practitioner Certification and even higher ranking skill levels than that.

At this point founders Richard Bandler and John Grinder have gone separate ways to each pursue the pot of gold at the end of the rainbow of their choice. Yet each continues to add to the repertoire of the technology. Bandler seems to have the reputed edge in creativity, but then taking sides in an issue like that is like arguing whether blondes or brunettes are better. (Don't press me for an answer.)

The Basics

To simplify things a little, this is what you are dealing with:

The NLP technology: human nature as it is experienced by all of us day-to-day is revealed. The subjective and objective person is demystified.

The NLP Training: How we think and feel and how we learn and change are revealed. Very explicit techniques to make things happen in human events that you never thought possible are now possible. (I hope you believe in the five-minute phobia cure; some of us do it every day.)

The NLP Applications: Wherever there are people, there is human nature, and there is also NLP in teaching, management, therapy, law, medicine, and more.

NLP is a discovery, not an invention. This is a crucial issue. Bandler and Grinder did not sit down and design a system like your average guru such as the fellows who invented est or Insight. They worked with people and discovered ways to change behavior that are simply astounding in long-range and short-term implications. They used scientific methods and got reproducible, scientific results—including the ability to tell you how to clone yourself into a charismatic guru if you have a mind to do so.

But there is a catch. The way they think about human nature is as different from conventional behavioral science as it is practiced now as the physics and relativity of Einstein was different from that of Newton. In fact, NLP is to behavioral science as Einstein is to physics. You have to be able to think in *relative* terms.

Einstein once asked a conductor, "What time does Zurich stop at this train?" This kind of reverse, Oriental logic is part and parcel of the NLP experience. It is a little jarring at first. Improvisational Theater actors have more of a sense of how it works than do traditional psychologists. You switch roles and improvise your lines frequently based on feedback from your audience.

These things are extremely basic to the "Nelper," yet I know how alien the ideas and terms can be. Fuzzy Functions and Complex Equivalence can be tedious to the newcomer. They were to me, too, just a couple of years ago and yet I am now sitting here amazed at just how easily all of this is learned. In fact my seventeen-year-old son, Ben, is a trainee at The Eastern NLP Institute (where I am Co-director) along with a host of Ph.D.s, M.D.s, and managers and professors and nutritionists and various other professional types.

He isn't doing the complex things I am doing, but he proves the technology can be learned by someone with a teenager's experience. He won't do certain things instantaneously as a person with more life experience would do, yet he is quite competent at the skills. (You ought to witness him talking me out of the keys to the Corvette.) The level of skills I now teach advanced students is a bit tougher and more demanding, but extraordinary in terms of what it lets them accomplish.

You might be more comfortable if you think of NLP in terms of some other kind of technology—say a computer. A computer is more complicated than a typewriter, but it makes life a lot easier. When you think about it, computers do some pretty amazing things, but they need you to command them. And so does NLP.

OK—Just what are the advantages of NLP? To really understand, you'd have to make a list of all the limitations of the dialogs you now have. That is not easy to do because it demands a very different way of understanding what goes on in a conversation. Most of us generally assume that a dialog with someone else already does what it is supposed to do, so our expectations of it and what we get match . . . and we don't expect any more than we get.

If for some reason a dialog doesn't go our way, we tend to think of the other person as the reason (i.e., it's their fault) rather than the communication media of the conversation itself. The "media" is: *How* we dialog—not *What* we say. The way you holler at the mountain is the way your echo comes back. This essentially means that we don't think of the short-comings of a conversation any more than we tended to think of the shortcomings of automobiles prior to the oil shortage. Our tendency was to take for granted that what automakers turned out as what we expected. After our expectations were shaken up by the Middle East, we tended to notice mileage, weight, size, and other things about cars we didn't consider before.

Once you came to expect high mileage, you may have wondered why Detroit never thought of it before. After comparing an NLP conversation with an ordinary conversation, I came to understand the limitations of the latter as being rather random and not very much under my own control in spite of what I had believed earlier. "Duologs" were the result, not dialogs.

When you're using NLP rationales in your thinking, you tend not to infer any sort of *reason* for the other person's comment, you notice instead their *behavior*— both verbal and nonverbal. Sir Laurence Olivier would figure the audience reaction as the effect his doings not their truculence. Suppose you are trying to convince the other person to go along with you on some line of thought and they persist in their own opinion. The clear indication is that you are not changing their mind. Most of us will want to figure out the reason for their stubbornness. Somehow we assume that it will be helpful to know the reason for their persistence. A better idea is to wonder how they hold that opinion and how you can say something relevant to change their mind.

Maybe it doesn't sound like a big difference, but the contrast of the non-useful *why* compared to the useful *how* makes all the difference in the world in having a means to change a mind. Even if you are able to get the person's answer to your "why" question, it will not give you the means to change their mind. Suppose you are trying to get your friend to stop smoking. Your friend will have a ready answer about why he or she smokes or why they cannot stop.

But then you are forced to notice that *habit overrides reason.* Therefore, the reasons are secondary conscious rationalizations to whatever unconscious mechanism drives the habit. And the simple fact is that the reasons people have for this sort of issue have nothing whatever to do with how the habit is maintained. These mechanisms are, by definition, unconscious; so it is of no use to ask for irrelevant conscious reasons unless you are at a loss for what to say next in the dialog.

NLP often bypasses consciousness to work at the unconscious level. So if you feel compelled to ask "why," you will get lots of irrelevant reasons. Go ahead if you must. Perhaps there will always be room for "filler material" in any conversation. But whether in casual conversation, therapy, training, meetings, or whatever medium you work, you will find questions like *"How* do you know *when* to do what," will get you a lot further a lot faster.

The New York Times ran an article on cognitive science "as a revolutionary new field of inquiry." NLP wasn't mentioned specifically—an index of its obscurity partly due to its founding by outsiders (a mathematician and a linguist).

But it is also an index of how hard it is to transition one's understanding to its *relative* premises. Unless one is able to make that breakthrough from absolute thinking to relative thinking, NLP is just so much bafflegab. NLP can train you to make the transition, but often one must convince the potential NLP student of the value of doing so. If you aren't "a natural," it can be a hard sell indeed.

Perfectly Simple

"Nelpers" do some pretty amazing things.

EXAMPLE: An obvious item is that people perceive the world through their five senses . . . sight, sound, touch, taste, and smell. Apparently, it is not obvious that people have preferences for which of the five senses they tend to use for thinking. If you are a visualizer, you tend not to notice much of the auditory phenomena around you. If you are feeling oriented, you tend to blot out perceptions that are loaded with visual or auditory characteristics.

Bandler and Grinder noticed that there are eye patterns that are UNIVERSAL IN THEIR OPERATION. When people look up they are making pictures in their mind. When they look horizontally, they are making sounds; and when down to the right (for righthanders), they are feeling something.

From this one discovery, which is quite elementary in NLP, at least a dozen doctoral dissertations have been generated. The practical applications of this one piece of information are procedures that can make spellers out of non-spellers in about twenty minutes, rapport can be enhanced by matching your own comments to the other person's preferred sensory system, and husbands and wives can find new ways of enjoying each other by matching the sensory system of their mates.

Business presentations can be convincing and riveting when the audience is appealed to with the procedures that grow out of this one simple discovery.

By noticing the rate of speech of your conversational partner, you can match it, and with casual effort, can lead the other person to important decisions that could not be possible by using common sense. The reason is that matching the speech or breathing patterns of the other person so drastically enhances rapport that virtually anything is possible in the interview if you have the related skills to use what you have wrought with rapport.

In other words, advanced students are hard put not to believe they can influence a common brick to express tears, so great is the effect of the technology.

Of course such things are neat tricks, but they are small justification for the growing reputation of NLP as the cats' whiskers of the psychological jet set. Beyond the emotional suffering that NLP routinely eliminates in painless and rapid ways, NLP shines at boosting the creative process. And that is surprising to many. It is referred to as "generative" change rather than remedial change. People can learn to generate novel innovations in their own capacity, abilities, and intelligence.

Virtually any aspect of human potential can be achieved with the methods that now exist. No doubt there is a darker side to all this. I noticed at one of the training programs that there were an awful lot of military intelligence officers in attendance. I can easily imagine "spooks" being programed to do amazing and dubious things in the name of national security. If Hitler had known of this, we could have been in real trouble. But we can't turn back the clock. NLP has been discovered. The technology is neutral. People are not.

CHAPTER TWO

THE ROLE OF THE CONSULTANT'S EGO

I once listened to a colleague who had a strong tendency to explain things to clients by using many personal experiences and stories that emerged out of the colleague's life. Certainly there is nothing wrong with using one's own experience to make a point. However, this particular colleague was something of a model of inappropriate use of personal references when explaining things.

When I carefully mentioned this tendency, the response was a gracious explanation of the "reasons" for his use of the first person in conversations of any type. His reasons were to my way of thinking rather irrelevant. The fact was that my friend had a bad habit of overusing the pronoun "I." I, to coin a word, was dismayed because he didn't notice that he was often losing his audience to anger and boredom with incessant personal references.

I tried an experiment to make a change in his behavior. Some psychologists maintain that if a person is overdosed with a particular stimulus they will tire of it and want a change. Well, the theory didn't hold up in this case in spite of the fact that it worked that way on his clients. At any rate, this is what I did.

I typed up a sheet of paper covering the entire page with several paragraphs of

IIIIIIIIIIIIIIIIIIIIIIIIIIIIIIIIIIIIIIIIIIIIIIIIIIIIIIIIIIIIIIIIIIIIIIIII
IIIIIIIIIIIIIIIIIIIIIIIIIIIIIIIIIIIIIIIIIIIIIIIIIIIIIIIIIIIIIIIIIIIIIIIII
IIIIIIIIIIIIIIIIIIIIIIIIIIIIIIIIIIIIIIIIIIIIIIIIIIIIIIIIIIIIIIIIIIIIIIIII

"What's this?," he asked when handed such a long list of personal pronouns.

"That," I said, "is my estimate of the number of times you use the personal pronoun I in the course of your average dialog. I thought you'd like to know how important this technique is in your work." Being of pure motives I was thinking of a carpenter I had once heard of who went to work one day and was stunned to be turned away from the job. The boss advised the carpenter that he had recklessly used up too many inches the day before. As a result, he didn't have enough inches left over to continue the work. If one can use too many inches, I reasoned, maybe my friend could use too many I's. Surely there is a government regulation on the fair use of pronouns and my friend could have been at risk of using up his allotted quota. I explained that I didn't want him to put his work in jeopardy since he was so obviously sincere. My point was not well taken.

In pondering the response, I realized with 20/20 hindsight that my approach may have been ill-conceived. Ego is necessary for any professional as a source of confidence and independence. Presuming we have something to say presumes it is important. Otherwise why would professionals even exist? Obviously, I hadn't sufficiently softened my words to avoid bruising my friend's ego.

He truly felt he had something to say and personal experience for him was a form of speaking from the heart. No doubt it was an authentic feeling. But feelings are not the measure of reality. After all, members of the Flat Earth Society feel strongly that the round earth notion is an elaborate hoax.

His reality should have properly been the client's reality. He was losing the client and that was a clue to do something else besides telling stories that were of interest to himself instead of to his client. Relating personal experience was a good ploy but not an "all-purpose" ploy to be used all of the time. My hope had been to persuade him to reference someone else some of the time. After all, one's personal experiences can't cover all the bases. Experience is bigger than any single person's life. Even the *New York Times* and *National Enquirer* will go so far as to quote a source, so why couldn't my friend do the same?

Naturally, there are appropriate uses. A book like this one, for instance, is a good place. Frequently I use the first person as I did from the very first word of this chapter. When I communicate about firsthand experience as a consultant (often) or as a therapist (sometimes), the use of the first person makes sense. At other times it doesn't carry the point as well to the audience. Whoever you are helping, it may boil down to an issue of style.

But style is measured, ultimately, by its effects. You don't HAVE to avoid the first person in one kind of dialog. Nor do you HAVE to use it in another. The simple fact is that you can do anything and get away with it . . . if you do it with skill that affects your audience in the desired ways.

My grade school English teachers were evangelistic about suppressing the use of "I" in order to avoid boring the audience and to amplify the involvement of the target audience. We know, of course, there are communication techniques that allow both self and audience plenty of room in the dialog. It is not an either/or situation.

Yet that rather formal approach to English helped counter the tendency of all of us to do what my friend was doing . . . talking to himself instead of to his audience. My English teacher's suppression of self represents the opposite swing of the pendulum.

The worst part of the formal approach to suppressing the communicator is found in scientific circles. There one finds in full bloom the pretense that one is more objective by communicating in articles and speeches as though one were a disembodied voice from the sky presenting intelligent facts. It makes a discussion as exciting as reading an auto parts cata-log or a train schedule. It gives the illusion that the facts exist independent of the author when it is the author who selects and emphasizes or downplays the facts he or she wants to use.

All perception is selective. That means it is a question of the effects you want that determine your choice of tools to achieve them. This includes judicious use of the pronoun "I." I, for one, believe this is important to know.

Opinion is fertile territory for the first person. But a profes-sional communicator such as a consultant, executive, teacher or therapist, is usually solicited for useful expertise as opposed to value-laden opinion. Sharing personal stories, anecdotes and other personally referenced material is merely the pack-age for an audience-targeted message.

For example, jokes are peppered through many a profes-sional's dialog to make a point, not merely to achieve a few ego strokes for being funny. Communicators use techniques like "reframes" and "isomorphic metaphors" with the sort of cal-culated procedures and techniques employed by surgeons for a specific result. If delivered in the first person there should be good reason.

Plain description might be considered more objective by some—but we know better. Even in eliciting client issues there is a bias determined by what we are trained to notice. Despite the absence of the first person in other communication modes and styles, it is not hard to figure the viewpoint of the professional. There are always giveaways in what is noticed and what is not noticed or communicated. Indeed, the Rever-end Jerry Falwell could find sexual innuendos in the afore-mentioned train schedule.

Obviously a communicator is trained to assume that there is even communication in the absence of communication. The practitioner is the vicarious ears and eyes of the client. So we hear and see what he or she intends. The practitioner man-ages information for intended effects. Ask anyone subjected to an interview by *60 Minutes* about loaded viewpoints.

As stationery can communicate as much as the writing, so does the form of communication often tell us as much as the content of the message. When a practitioner asks about, say, family as opposed to career, we are learning something about the asker's priorities and we might even anticipate the choice of technique to follow.

It's virtually impossible to hide viewpoint, but you shouldn't concern yourself about it as a communicator. No one expects objectivity . . . and it's not even a goal. A communicator by definition has something to say that represents one aspect of reality at the expense of those aspects left out. Good work assumes selection of technique to achieve a given outcome. Without a message, there is no earthly reason to communicate in the first place. Punk rock may be an exception.

Presuming there is an idealist in even the most practical of us, subjectivity is unavoidable which makes it reality. The goal then is not objectivity or fairness: The goal is, rather, awareness of effects.

With that framework, let's return to the issue of the first person. The use of self-disclosure is a much-discussed issue in professional circles. As you would expect that means guideline questions are raised which you might ask yourself.

— Is my personal experience relevant enough to the clients' goals to wrap it in a technique such as a long metaphor?

— Will I be able to keep my distance from the material so that I continue to observe if the client response is what I want?

— Will my selection of delivery technique ensure that the client gets the intended meaning instead of getting bored with egotistical verbal "home movies" about me?

These are not easy questions to answer. But I could run out of fingers and toes several times over counting the number of times it was obvious my colleagues did not answer those questions before they began work with a client. Still, style is a marvelously complex thing and those with effective style can utilize anything well and make it work. So what if it turns out to be the only way they can do it—if it works? If you are one of those professionals and it works for you, you are going to do it anyway. You have my blessing.

Maybe I say that because subjective experience is ultimately all there is anyway. After all, all reality is stored in the grey matter right alongside the *Monday Night Football* scores and memories of my first sexual experience. Nonetheless I can abandon the first person. Talking to an audience of scientists is an example of matching their rules and notions of "objective" ways of phrasing ideas. It wouldn't matter that the ideas were constructed by my very own, usually operational, subjective brain and presented selflessly by my very own subjective ego. It wouldn't matter that I was reporting MY efforts and MY results. It would matter that IF it works as part of the story, make it part of the story.

On another tack, if I don't work in the first person, will anything suffer? A common reframe I use with employees of major corporations will serve as an example. Many employees rationalize the company policy as being benevolent, forgiving and tolerant of below-par performance—especially if it is their own. And very especially if they have reasons (I call them excuses) such as personal problems, insensitive colleagues and unsuccessful past lives for those into reincarnation. How would you deliver the message: "If you don't perform you will be fired?"

Using the first person approach I might say this: "I was once in a similar situation. My mom always told me that my self-worth was never to be questioned. Personally, I liked my work but not the . . ." and so on. Maybe it would work and maybe it wouldn't.

Conversely, using the client as the touchstone I might try my famous "Mercenary Reframe." "Do you think of yourself as an employee?" I ask. Then I ask "Why do you bother to come here to work?" After some judicious leading the response is: "For money of course." "As a consultant," I add, "it is clear that if I don't perform, I'm not invited back the next day." Notice that I have sneaked in a couple of mentions of myself. "Because you are not a consultant you feel secure in having a salary, right?"

After an affirmative response from them, I snap back "WRONG! It is an illusion that you are an employee. You are a consultant just like I am. It merely takes a little longer for you to get uninvited." If the delivery catches their attention —and it always does—I then administer the *coup de grace*. "The simple fact is that you sell your body and brain to this organization to solve their problems. YOU are in fact a MER-CENARY hired to shoot down problems and if you don't, YOU are going to be shot down!"

Take it for granted that I do this with style. It works like a charm to change the dependent complainer into a willing participant in cleaning up his or her act. But the key difference is that I refer to their reality and their situation and their illusions—not mine. It makes a difference, believe me. I have tried it both ways and it works better if I leave out my I.

The client will never ask for the validation of whether it has ever happened to me. The client is busy working his issues. It is taken for granted that I am there in the other chair. Do I really need to be noticed? It would be worth wearing socks with holes if I can deliver this message to you: If you can, do it the second way and make it work. The big advantage is that you get to pay more attention to your role as professional observer. You get to be the resource. You are the vicarious eyes and ears of the client by meeting his needs. Isn't that what you are being paid for? (Ha! I snuck it in—YOU are a mercenary too, and if you don't shoot down client problems vs. shooting off your mouth you aren't doing your job.)

As a session progresses you may find yourself having an insight or even—it pains me to say it—forming an opinion that you think should be expressed. Well, O.K., it is wonderful that you are thinking. Go ahead, let the client know what's on your mind as long as you consciously select the way you package it. Compare questions to opinions, for example. You might ask, "Is such and so a fact? Or, Ugh, you might say, "I think ..." Kidding aside, CHOOSE your method. I'm not suggesting that you disassociate to the extreme of sounding like *Star Trek's* Mr. Spock ... "As a disinterested and neutral observer, one might suggest that a committee of peers would consider the following evidence as indicative of your neural functioning." Let's just take it for granted you have something to say.

So say it and make sure it works. Somehow, you will factor your presence into the message. Again, my message is: choose your technique on the basis of its effects.

Now let's cope with the issue of hidden agendas. Communicators often—no, usually—have them. You may be exploring the use of a new technique. You may secretly dislike the client's quirky little idiosyncracies. The client may present an issue about which you feel woefully inadequate to manage but your macho streak paralyzes your ability to speak the words: "What the heck is a 'frantzrab' anyway?" If it's a client issue big enough to present for your expertise, it also has the potential to be utilized to generate a big change.

If the client presents it to you to solve, he expects a relevant response. If you draw a blank, you don't have to say, "I apologize." You can always utilize the way they brought up the issue as a viable way to end-run your ignorance yet keep the process moving right along. If you do, you are going to make your client happy. Again it's a case of not referencing yourself, but the client.

No matter the nature of the issue, "point of view" is important. Award-winning points of view are those that don't preach like a minister, don't seem as pompous as a Porsche 928 owner or don't seem as one-sided as a Mobius Strip. No matter how good your personal experience is, it won't have a good effect if you sound like the latest reincarnation of Narcissus.

I repeatedly find that a happy way to present an opinion, if

I must, is in the form of a question and in the contextual framework of it being only one point of a continuum of positions ranging from pro to con.

Actually I perceive my perceptions as testable notions or hypotheses, not as opinions. An opinion doesn't have to be right. The Constitution says so. But a professional intervention had better be based on a lot more than the usual arbitrary feelings that are the bases of your average opinion.

If you are going to lead clients—and you are paid to lead clients—to some change of mind, rest easy on the fact that you are indeed manipulating their minds in the best way possible. That is, manipulate towards the payoff they want and in ways that are ecological to their values. You don't soften manipulation with apologies or by being a "wimp" and reporting personal experience as some form of inevitable divine inspiration delivered in the first person. Be unique. Tell them you are going to do things to their heads that they may never comprehend. But so what? Any decent physician, lawyer, or IRS agent will affect them with rather less concern for educating the person than for getting the job done.

You are paid for results. Let your expertise show if you must . . . "Well, sir, I'd like to do a six-step reframe and some embedded commands on you. Do you mind?" At least your clients will sense that you are someone to be trusted and most likely will go along with your program. Clients have the gift of second sight and they know an incongruity when they see one. Don't kind them with personalized baloney. And don't kid yourself. Even *Star Trek*'s Mr. Spock was proficient at rapport skills in spite of his distant demeanor.

By now you have noticed that "I" can be the proverbial nail that loses the shoe, the horse, the rider and the battle. "I" can be an intrusion, a source of distrust and the means for losing a client in extreme cases of overuse. After all, whose side are you on if all you do is mentally masturbate your own ego? Your chances are better if you walk a mile in their moccasins.

In the end, the bottom line is a matter of observation, technique and effects. Remember rules are made to be broken; try these on for size:

— Use the first person when it produces the effect you want.

— Avoid it if it doesn't match the client's situation or the specific process and strategy you are managing.

— Use it if there is no other resource handy or your experience is relevant and totally unique.

— Use it if you want to pull rank and let the client know who is in charge of the session.

Remember, the first person is a powerful tool. It is authoritative; it is the validation of personal experience; it is the means to bear witness. And it is also the means for transferring athlete's foot to the mouth.

CHAPTER THREE

ON BEING RELATIVELY ILLOGICAL

People think other people are illogical. And they are right. That is, the other person is illogical compared to yourself. But, on the other hand, you are illogical from their perspective. Willie Sutton, the famous bank robber, was asked why he robbed banks. The reporter's logic was no doubt framed to elicit some hidden psychological meaning in Willie's motivation. In that context, Willie's uniquely illogical response was, "Because that's where the money is!"

In the computer world there is an analogy to illustrate what this means. Languages like COBOL or PASCAL or BASIC are each logical within the context of their appropriate computer. Yet none of the languages will work on another piece of hardware unless there is some means of translation between them to make communication possible.

Human thinking is also illogical out of context. Your spouse may think having your in-laws over for a long visit is pleasant. Yet it might seem very illogical to you for another person to find pleasure in such a situation. The context of your spouse is not necessarily the same as yours. Thinking occurs within a context, purpose or frame of reference that is unique to the individual. If you don't know the context of another's thinking, many things can seem illogical. We all know politicians quote one another out of context and careers are won or lost on the impact of the message.

When you think of what you want for dinner, you think in terms of the context of where (location), with whom or when (time) or even in terms of good nutrition (biochemistry). These are all contextual factors. Yet the definition of a context is typically subjective. Let's take time as an example of context (though we could use motion, location, distance, importance, height, depth, and any of a host of other factors).

For example, some people think of time mostly in the past tense. Others think in the present tense or the future tense and still others switch back and forth in all three modes or combinations of them like an amphibian. This characteristic is a learned preference and it "frames" the range of behaviors that is possible within that subjective context. In this sense, a context is a set of limits that defines what is and, reciprocally, defines what is not at issue.

Context is a stabilizing reference point that locates where you are or are not in your subjective world. If an individual habitually thinks in terms of precedent (the past tense), it will be difficult for the person to imagine "possibilities" (future tense) if history isn't "imagined" into the "changed future." This type of phenomenon has a direct application to techniques we practitioners routinely use, such as a "changed history" or "changed future," when we work in either of those verb tenses.

The present tense tends to work well with the application of other techniques such as reframes. In the cases where a feeling limits a person's responses, we often separate the feeling from the other imagery in the mind to eliminate the negative kinesthetic, i.e., a bad feeling. To shift from technical to everyday jargon, I think of hope as a positive kinesthetic (Ki+), worry as a negative kinesthetic (Ki−), and realistic as a neutral kinesthetic.

When we contextualize (or conceptualize) stimuli in habitual ways there is a loss of behavioral response potential. A person who never looks backward in time can repeat unnecessarily the mistakes of history. While the person who never looks forward in time can't imagine new outcomes (say, an IRS agent trying to imagine less taxes). Habitual patterns that are contextually invariable act on behavior in a way that is similar to a sailing ship whose captain doesn't know how to sail against the wind. He can only sail if the wind is at his back, so sailing in any chosen direction is out of the question.

You can only do what your skills allow. If you are ever stuck a mile or so from shore in a Sunfish or Hoby Cat in shark-infested waters with the wind blowing you out to sea and you don't know how to sail against the wind, you will learn a new definition of panic.

Changes in response are not based on universally shared logic. They are based on subjective or idiosyncratic logic. Although the structure of subjective logic is universal, the content of the logic is not universal due to individually unique experience and memory.

Changes in the Frame Of Reference

As a generalization, having behavioral potential or flexible behavior means having many available responses to a given stimulus (the multiple choice of life!)

In our sailing example, we have at least two choices in thinking about adding behavioral alternatives. One is to add a specific behavior, such as learning how to sail into the wind. Another is to change the frame of reference entirely and decide if sailing is the transportation mode of choice. One might opt for submarines, swimming or aircraft depending on the purpose at hand. There are always options, it seems, if we know how to think of them.

Let's consider an everyday situation where changing the frame of reference spontaneously changes the behavior that is elicited by the same stimulus. Take a moment and fill in your response to the following incomplete sentence. "I'm happy when _____.

Whatever answer you used, it was a result of your perception of what it meant and your implicit definition of the frame of reference you were thinking in at that moment. Other situations would define the context differently so that your answer would be very different. Let's use the same sentence stem and vary the frames a bit.

How would you answer: "I'm happy when _____ " under each of these circumstances?

- You are discussing marriage plans with someone you love: "I'm happy when: *I'm near you, sweetheart.*"
- You are being interviewed for a high-paying executive job: "I'm happy when: *results are above standards.*"
- You are being treated by a psychologist for depression: "I'm happy when: *I sense I'm getting better and I can cope.*"

In each of these items we have the same stimulus producing a different response that depends on the frame we use to perceive the meaning. So the logic goes like this: The same stimulus equals the same response each time unless the context or frame changes. Then the result is that the same stimulus produces a different response. The phenomenon of how Anchors produce an "instant replay" gives an interesting extension of the idea that responses are more repetitious than we usually believe to be the case.

Anchoring, i.e., the notion of an instant conditioned response, helps us by providing the tool for producing an instant replay of any given response. This means that the anchor must be contextualized for it to produce the same response if that is what we need.

Conversely, if we want a different response from the same stimulus, all we need do is change the context and we get an instant change. A classic example of the latter is when a subordinate "badmouths" the boss in private, but says very different things in the immediate context of the boss.

A Model

A model I use to think about these issues is a typical "decision tree" that finds use in many disciplines such as management and data processing. The well-known stimulus response (SR) of behavioral science is a one-dimensional form of expression. The SR model does not cover the multiplicities of frames and responses in our clinical experience so I merge the SR and "decision tree" models as basic tools. These are the notational elements I use:

Stimulus = S

Response = R

i   =   a subscript for internal thinking responses (conscious or unconscious) (internal thoughts are also stimulus)

e   =   a subscript for external events (either stimulus or response)$(+0-)$ is another facet of the subscripts. I find it useful to categorize the responses occurring in terms of another modeling component. All responses can be "scored" for kinesthetic value of positive $(+)$ neutral (0) or negative $(-)$. I blend that into the model too. This is based on the TACS model (see glossary) that illustrates that a great deal of clinical work involves separating kinesthetic images from visual, auditory, olfactory and gustatory imagery. That is, we neutralize an undesirable feeling that "piggybacks" on other types of images.

Following is an illustration of how the model looks on paper. Each horizontal line represents a potential behavioral response. It is useful to imagine that there might be as many potential behavioral responses as people could think into existence. The five response options shown here are purely arbitrary for the sake of illustration, and any of them could be kinesthetically positive, neutral or negative. Of course there could potentially be an infinity of choices if we needed to think them up.

A habit is the case where the same response repeats invari-

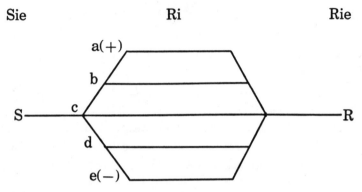

ably to the same stimulus leaving the person, as it were, with no choices. For example, every time some folks see a magazine centerfold at the newsstand the response is very much the same. The longest horizontal line "c" could represent that habitual response.

Of course, it would not always be appropriate to drool so obviously in public so we might want to install a neutral response, say, "b" or "d" in case one's spouse is nearby . . . just for the sake of family harmony. Possibly, we might want to add a strong positive response, "a," if it helps one get "psyched up" for happy bedroom activities.

The NLP task is to add choices. We like to make people "choosey." One of those choices is to determine if the frame of reference should be changed as one of the behavioral options. Comedians change frames on us to get laughs; the classic joke of conversationally saying, "Take my wife. PLEASE! Take my wife!" For a client, however, I often want to install a habit of choice—a compelling choice that is a well-formed outcome for them.

One of the ways I change the behavior from habit to choice is, paradoxically, to install a compulsion for choosing the optimum response at the right time. I may do this in any situation where I want highly leveraged change, such as in a Meta Model violation or a stultifying belief that limits behavioral alternatives.

An illustration of the seemingly illogical "same stimulus

cue/different response" is given to us by C. S. Dweck and B. G. Licht in *Learned Helplessness and Intellectual Achievement.* You will find it in M.E.P. Seligman and J. Garber, the editors of *Human Helplessness: Theory and Research* (New York: Academic Press 1980). In this case, the difference in individual responses is a function of differences in the internal programming of the children who were studied in the project.

Dweck and Licht compared the different responses of children to solving puzzles of discrimination and logic of the sort used in aptitude and achievement tests. Initially, all the children performed at the same level of ability. They were comparable in tests of accuracy, speed, and effectiveness of problem-solving strategy.

At a key dividing point, the fourtuples and strategies changed and sorted the children into two groups. When difficulty was encountered, some children's performance improved, while the performance of other children deteriorated. It would seem to be totally illogical to the average bystander that this should occur. The different fourtuples elicited by failure are instructive and alert us about how the internal responses are different even though the stimulus was the same.

These differences also give us an idea of useful approaches to managing the problems of the helpless by taking a cue from the more successful strategy of the contrasting group.

The Inner Experience of Success and Failure

The children achieved very different perceptions of themselves as a result of their experience on the tasks. The key determinants are largely the result of earlier "programming" which taught them about how to interpret the meaning of their experience. This was the source of the apparently illogical differences.

The children who perceived themselves as helpless had these characteristics:

— **Nominalizations:** they immediately label their difficulty as failure.

— **Cause and Effect:** Their logic attributes "failure" to lack of ability (e.g.," I have a lousy memory"). This is a Meta Model violation which is attacked with standard NLP procedures of Meta Model challenges.

— **Looping:** They stop correcting their mistakes. Instead they go round and round in their internal state of confusion. They become preoccupied with the mistakes instead of with alternative responses to the ones which didn't work.

— **Deletion:** They delete reference to their prior successes. The unconscious programming leads to a dead end of bad feeling and they then look for "reasons" which make sense to their limited conscious understanding of what is happening to them. They then act as though the conscious reasons are the actual determinants, which is clearly not the case.

— **Decision:** They consciously sense that their lack of ability is defined as irreparable since it is natural for them to feel that way after a bit of practice at having the feeling. Their immediate experience of difficulty elicits the familiar negative conditioned response.

— **Kinesthetics:** They attach negative feeling to neutral feedback about their efforts. "This isn't fun any more" is a typical response. Feedback is no longer simply information. Prior conditioning determines its meaning.

— **Alternatives:** They then put their attention into alternative environmental activities once they are unable to change their internal state. Since they "feel" they are unchangeable, they usually try to manipulate the environment to achieve relief.

— **Process:** They then score for failures and delete successes and the practice at feeling bad confirms their sense of failure.

Successful Strategies

Those who run into difficulty and overcome it have a different internal process. Here are their typical reactions:

-**Nominalizations:** They identify errors as temporary setbacks to be remedied quickly.

-**Looping:** They do not loop on mistakes: They interpret mistakes as information or as neutral feedback that instructs them about how to proceed.

-**Sorting:** They notice events as positive kinesthetic experience and do not label errors as failures with attendant bad feelings. They don't search for the cause of errors but for causes that will act as solutions.

-**Choice:** They think about how to develop alternative approaches that will work better than the ones they have tried so far.

-**Kinesthetics:** At the emergence of difficulty they elicit a positive kinesthetic at the challenge of the problem.

-**Future Pace:** They imagine a positive solution and pursue success in a self-induced behavior generator process.

-**Persistence:** They persist in the task since it is experienced as a positive feeling vs. a negative feeling that would tell them to stop. They are not handicapped with the interpretation of an obstacle as a time to feel bad and quit. They experience a limitation as a signal to do something different instead of as a signal to stop. Internal dialog tends to go along these lines: "I should slow down and figure this out," or "The harder it gets, the harder I need to try."

-**Cause and Effect:** At the lack of success, failure was cause and effect attributed to lack of effort, not to intrinsic limitations. At lack of success, no judgment was made of ability but of effort.

-**Sorting:** They noticed what worked for them and thus scored for successes.

After the task was over, the helpless children generalized the meaning and pervasiveness of failure which led them to forget successes and notice only losses, not gains. They future-paced failure in their thinking via the Ki-feeling associated with their imagination of the outcome.

The successful children thought they would succeed again. They future-paced with positive kinesthetics. The task could be approached as an installation of the success strategy into the children with the failure strategy.

Since helplessness or dependency is a pervasive phenomenon, the task of the practitioner is to find interventions that will assist helpless individuals who demonstrate this type of pattern. There are many ways to help.

Some change possibilities are as follows:
- Separate the negative kinesthetic from their future pacing and add Ki+'s
- Add a behavior generator to future pace Ki+s
- Add a persistence routine to developing alternatives with Ki+'s
- Model and clone the strategy of the successful children.
- Match submodalities of the positive kinesthetic imagery to their models
- Use reframes to change the meaning of "failure" and "scoring"
- Use a competitive reframe for the shy to help them approach solutions
- Remove fears of being judged and neutralize criticism phobias
- Shift them out of blame frame and "reasons" toward "results"
- Install a compulsion to develop Ki+ or neutral alternatives vs. Ki−s

Of course each individual will have unique aspects to his pattern. This calls for eliciting specific resources for each person individually.

This sort of limitation will express itself in various ways. The client may complain of compulsive feelings of inadequacy. If not meta-modeled to find out the triggering situations and strategy, one would not identify the structure of the pattern.

The way an internal conflict can appear is in wanting to succeed yet being inhibited by the negative kinesthetic associated with "failure." This consideration of the children's superficial "illogical differences" illustrates different ways a pattern can be identified and matched to an appropriate technique to effect the desired changes. The person needs the ability to stop the activity by choice (will power) versus being unhappily stopped by the limiting behavior.

Installing a Compulsion

One of the many ways to install successfully "choosy" behavior is to overcome the mindless use of the polarity response. All individuals are polarity responders in some contexts. That is, polarity responders will notice what is wrong (according to personal experience and ideals) before noticing what is right in their perceptions of reality. Problems will occur with inflexible polarity responses in anyone if the response is compulsive instead of appropriate.

There are ways to change a negative (polarity or reactive) person to a positive responder. (I assume that the range of possibilities are positive, neutral and negative. And I assume that the neutral perceiver is generally called a realistic person while the other two responses are usually called optimistic or pessimistic in nature.)

One method to mention briefly is regression. Childhood has times when natural curiosity and positive expectations (future pacing) is the norm rather than the exception. Childhood is a time when there are many exciting *firsts that are perceived as fun.* For example, the first rollercoaster ride, meeting the first celebrity, the first airplane trip and so on.

The main method suggested here is to elicit such a positive state for new situations or information and to bring the state into the present with a shift in strategy-triggers and to cue the anchors to the future pacing, too. The result is to make new ideas potentially pleasant instead of generating the "not invented here" polarity response.

Another more conversational (and less formal) approach is to use the following recipe:

- Ask the person to describe the current pattern of negative sorting to anchor the fourtuple.
- Alternatively, you might simply and casually lead them into noticing and agreeing with your description of the pattern by feeding their behavior back to them (in a positive frame, of course) and get them into a "yes" set of mind. "So it is true that you are having some difficulty?" will positively pace a negative experience.
- Explain that the polarity pattern has real usefulness. An example is the school play ground bully who pushes people around until he goes one push too far and the pushee polarizes and gives the bully a karate chop to the nose. A positive value of the reactive polarity pattern is that it triggers protective behavior. The typical subjective experience of polarity responders is that they are harder to fool or to trick.
- A metaphoric explanation is to describe the period of a million years ago when homo sapiens ran around the African veldt in shoulder-high grass looking for something to eat. As a rule all the grass would wave uniformly in the wind in the same back-and-forth motion. However, a patch of grass that stays curiously still is the exception and that is where the tiger is sitting, waiting to catch the person for its dinner. In essence, you explain the need to perceive by exception is crucial and cannot be dismissed out of hand. It has real survival value. But it needs to be done when appropriate and not compulsively all the time.
- Then ask the client to look around the room. Lead them to notice colors, line form, texture, light, furniture, etc.

- Then, ask them if they noticed any light switches (or lightbulbs, doorknobs or telephones as best fits your plan).
- Then, congruently, tell them that it is now their pattern to notice the light switch every time they come into a room and to think of the moment going on right now (anchoring the change dialog to the everyday anchor of the light switch that will trigger off the memory each time they see one). This presupposes that they will notice the anchor and, in fact, they do.
- Each time they experience the anchor, you tell them, they will then have to choose if they want to sort negatively or positively.

This way you have installed a compulsion to choose instead of the habit of sorting negatively. You may also want to presuppose a clock or calendar in the rationale. Instruct them that they will notice the compulsive phenomenon for a day, a week, a month, etc. And tell them that after that time, the awareness will drop out of consciousness to operate fully and automatically on cue.

Of course, there are many other possibilities. For example, we could also use a submodality approach to illogical behavior. Following is a case where a woman had some persistent negative moods associated with childhood experiences. The change of installing alternate moods was achieved—but not easily.

Submodality Recipe

I had achieved some dramatic changes in the effects of childhood traumas associated with medical treatment that was quite frightening. I'd used a variety of techniques. But when I tried to future pace the changes with this client I ran into an unexpected issue . . . the client's beliefs interfered with the installation.

The client did not believe that such a painful, lifelong issue could be resolved so easily—even though the "unconscious" agreed that it was completed as evidenced by the nonverbal signals elicited from a modified six-step reframe.

I decided to use a submodality in a different way. Using the contrast frame I asked the client to tell me a small lie, to make up some fictitious story about what had been done earlier in the day (i.e., going to the store to buy me a dozen doughnuts —which had never happened). The critical submodalities were color (monochrome) and location (simultaneous visual construct and auditory construct with the visual being most in consciousness).

The contrast submodality I elicited was for the "laughing place" which was in visual and in auditory recall. This spot was also kinesthetically anchored to a finger to add credibility for the client since it was not especially necessary for the procedure.

A relationship the client had with a boyfriend was the focal point for the future pace. The client could not imagine a good relationship emerging with her boyfriend. She was asked to imagine it in an "as if" frame, i.e., to make it up while the eyes were in the position of the manufactured lie. That way it was easy to imagine that the situation could be better. Then the "constructed lie" about a wonderful relationship was replayed in the "laughing place" and it got some laughs and it seemed to be a factual reality. It worked.

Then another aspect to the situation appeared. She kept describing her situation in the past tense as if the changed history that had just reorganized her experience was still very real and current. Many of those memories were then replayed in the "lie" location, which made them seem very unreal and of little impact on her life. She was given a series of these memories to play in the "lie" location and they covered a great many of the situations that were likely to occur in the near future.

In other words, all of her hallucinations seemed real to her so they were put into an image processing location that made them not seem so important and which got her out of her past and into the future.

Initially she was Meta Modeled using the McClelland model against a series of situations or contexts. It is named after David McClelland, the Harvard psychologist who first studied these three motives. The model sorts for three important motives, i.e., power, affiliation and achievement. She had been observed to be implicitly describing her situation as a conflict between being dependent and independent, which are intimately tied up with the motives studied by David McClelland. Of course, this conflict was related to historical life incidents and she replayed the pattern repeatedly and pervasively in her life, i.e., with men, with work, with herself and with almost every imaginable context except for children and old folks and clients.

Those exceptions did not cause her to polarize since she was in power in those situations. She had experienced the other types of people as untrustworthy and undependable. So I penciled the following illustration on a scrap of paper.

By asking her to spread 100 imaginary points down each column, it gave a map of her various motives as elicited in each of those contexts. Adding this information to the Yeager Power Grid (YPG) provided the conclusion that she was deleting the interdependent mid-portion of the scale of the YPG (as defined below) on a scale of one to ten.

Those facts, together with her own descriptions of her polarity response pattern to virtually anything in relationships, provided the leverage for the 80/20 rule, i.e., that the leverage for 80% of her problems was the 20% that she was not addressing in her content descriptions of her situations and symptoms.

	self	men	job	clients	old folks	kids
n POW	___	___	___	___	___	___
n AFF	___	___	___	___	___	___
n ACH	___	___	___	___	___	___
100pts	( )	( )	( )	( )	( )	( )

It was a case of what she was NOT saying that was revealed by the McClelland model. Noticing her deletions of the mid-portion of the YPG and the effects of her pervasive polarity response gave my thinking the leverage for change. I found an important clue to the validity of her strong motivation to change. She was only limited by the lack of "how to" skills that a practitioner could provide.

The clue was her consistency in not having chosen an emotionally comfortable career but unchallenging career of working with children or old folks. Though she had worked in such jobs, and even though they were comfortable, those situations would not be ultimately satisfying. She sensed those jobs would not help her solve the chronic problem of being limited by her patterns.

The Yeager Power Grid is a simplified and powerful model of human interactions. If you can imagine the standard "scale of 1 to 10," her patterns were expressed by extremes. As illustrated below consider that "one" on the scale is a passive, dependent, Charlie Brown and "five" is assertiveness such as found in Alan Alda of *M.A.S.H.* fame and "ten" is an aggressive, independent and punitive mode. She spent her emotional time flip-flopping between the extremes of "one" and "ten" depending on the contextual cues that would trigger her pattern. She associated the lists of events below with each of these states.

She basically made a binary reality. Her world was a state of either dependent or independent. There was no interdependence. This was a clear case of Yeager's "wrong category." A continuous definition of her reality would have been

1	5 Assertive Interdependent	10
(1)Charlie Brown/dependent-		(10)Attila the Hun/independent
hospitalization		jobs that kept people at a distance
hurtful physicians		quitting situations that crowded her
operations and pain		withdrawing from others to keep distance
stepfather relationship		psychosomatic illness as distancing
rejection by peers		a strong distrust of people in general
need for closeness		a distrust of anyone who seemed OK to her

more useful than her either/or definition. She emotionally was put in many dependent situations where she had to rely on or attempt to obtain support from adults who, in the past, consistently did not meet her basic childhood needs for assistance. She had many such in situations calling for adult guidance and nurturance as a child and was consistently left in the lurch.

As a result, she had either not developed or had deleted the category of "interdependent." She learned not to trust anyone to help her, yet she wanted to trust and have close relationships. Because of the conflict, she alternated between the extremes of the scale of the Yeager Power Grid, vacillating between Charlie Brown (dependent) and Attila the Hun (in her case, a very aggressive independence which was also connected to her sense of pride). She had virtually deleted the entire mid-range set of responses of "interdependency" where most folks want and need to be most of the time.

As she would get into situations eliciting either Charlie Brown or Attila the Hun responses from her, she would polarize and go into the frame of the opposite end of the scale. She spent her time vacillating between dependence and independence and polarizing as she entered either. It made for a moody existence and lots of negative kinesthetics.

It also produced transient relationships, since they all had time bombs built into them as a result of her presuppositions that others could not be depended upon. This expectation also combined to bias her perceptions as a classic self-fulfilling prophecy since she inadvertently arranged them all to fail.

Also in her search for satisfaction of this emotional itch to get her act together, she tried virtually every self-help, holistic or religious program available. This pattern of restless searching is a good index of the desire of any individual to change their own patterns. It is a powerful index of their need for help. The search for this kind of positive change is a compulsive act. At times, I think it is an instinct for growth.

A good parallel example is the seriously overweight person

whose motivation is applied to eating. Imagine if the same energy were channeled in other directions . . . the fatter, the more motivated.

I often tell a particular "dog story" to elicit the readiness for a full range of responses over the "scale of ten" as described above. If someone, as a child, is bitten in the diaper by a large dog and gains a phobia of dogs, it precludes the person enjoying the petting of a neighbor's dog or the possibility of owning a guard dog if desired.

On the scale of ten, the phobia would be a "one", the cautious approach to a friend's dog a "five" and having a pet dog a "ten". The phobic response would preclude the entire range of alternate responses. The individual is led to want to have access to the full range of responses and not to be limited.

As in the dog story set up, her "part" was elicited to confirm the situation as it was portrayed to her. It agreed. It also agreed to let go of the signal that was trying to catch her attention negative kinesthetics. The part was periodically asked for confirmation as the above process went along. She shifted from asymmetrical expressions of gesturing with the left hand to the symmetrical gesturing of both hands. She was fixed.

In Summary

Since we started out discussing illogical behavior, the above client's responses to others were certainly experienced as illogical. Flip-flopping moods, temper tantrums and transient relationships were all the result of being stuck in a subjective wilderness without choice. The children mentioned in the earlier study showed also that what seems illogical to the bystander is logical if you find the uniqueness in the person.

Once a person's unique definitions of reality are elicited, however, the situation virtually always comes down to a case of "no choice." When clients come to practitioners for assistance, the one sure thing is that we will be searching for a way to help the individual choose more satisfying responses.

The result of examining this issue of illogical behavior is simple and profound. Reality is relative, not absolute. Emotional logic is relative to the perceiver. The practitioner adds choice at the point where the person is presented with a stimulus and elicits, for the client, a new response potential in his or her repertoire. Now, isn't all this perfectly logical?

CHAPTER FOUR

SALES JOB

Good morning, class.

Good morning, sir.

Recently, I found myself thumbing through Frank Bettger's classic *How I Raised Myself From Failure to Success Through Selling*. Ordinarily, in my learning curve, I would not have considered myself a salesperson. Bettger changed my mind. I would like to change yours.

Now, class, many of you are probably wondering why I was fingering my way through such an alien type of literature. Ah, yes, Rachel. You may stop nodding your head now. I'm glad you wondered what I was thinking. Rachel? Are you awake?

Huh?! Oh, yes, I'm awake.

Of course I did not consider myself in sales. I still don't. Paradoxically, I am in sales even though I am not.

That sounds confusing, sir.

If you please, Rachel. I'm not trying to confuse the class. It has to do with the definition of what you mean by the notion of salesmanship. For me, the word conjures up images of mustachioed, slick-haired, used-car salesmen with a cardboard smile as wide as the Mississippi River. I have learned a new set of images that are a bit more flattering, now that I have joined the fold of those who do selling.

I have learned from Bettger that a salesman's prime task is to find a need and to help the other person fill that need. That definition fits almost everyone almost every day. If you hold a job, the corporation that employs you was sold on your value or you wouldn't have been selected for the job. The company had a need and you filled it.

That also applies to consultants and therapists. Your clients have needs and if you have a service, you can fill their needs. Not to mention, your loved ones have needs and often you attempt to sell them on your own version of the best way for them to satisfy those needs.

Yes, Benjamin, I'll get to that point right now. There is selling and there is selling. The way Bettger frames the situation is this: Imagine that you have a sign tatooed inside your forehead and it reads "How can I help you?" That one piece of advice has done an enormous amount of good for me and others to whom I have modestly conveyed the same message. What does the person want that they can't manage to obtain on their own?

In the helping professions, there seems to be some sort of scoring system that rates a therapist as more sincere if they downgrade the so-called "crass" business of selling their service. Some of that attitude comes from trying to be as sought-after as physicians are by posing as though money is not an important part of the equation of being a professional.

But a really competent helping professional is selling in each and every session that is conducted with a client. As we will learn, it is partially a matter of context that defines whether some folks consider an activity selling or not.

Sir, do you mean that persuasion is a factor in all human interactions?

A good question, Benjamin. I suspect you have been thinking about this topic. Well, the news is this: NLPing is a sales job and every successful NLPer is consciously or unconsciously a salesperson. It is my observation that most human encounters involve the attempt to influence the behavior of others whether in large matters or small. In essence selling, to me, is the desire to change another person's mind from one state to another. Often it is the desire to change someone from a resistant "No" to a happy "Yes."

Could you give us an example, sir?

Of course. Consider what you are doing when you tell a metaphor. You are asking a client to give you their time and attention. Not an easy task. You are assuming that the client believes that your story is relevant to his or her situation, that the story will directly or indirectly fill some aspect of their perceived needs . . . even though you may be very oblique in your delivery. How do you get the client to sit still for something that may not seem entirely relevant to his or her needs at the time? You sell them. Many times you will not think of it that way. But you have done something that keeps them glued to the dialog with you.

What, you may ask, is it that you do that could be considered selling? The answer is easy. You are in a context where the client believes that you are able to be of help. That's basic according to Bettger. But more to the point of your deliberate attempts to influence the client, you are explaining something of interest to them. A salesperson explains how one choice is more helpful than another. You are selling the person on a change of habit, perhaps, and that is a whole lot tougher sale than brooms, mops and brushes. (I once did that as a summer job.)

Adding choices to a client's repertoire of responses is a sales job from step one. You must gain rapport. You must lead effectively. You must chain together images in a precise and viable way to change their mind. By definition, your job is to change their mind. That is also what a salesperson does. And it is all done with words. Amazing.

Are you leading up to telling us a story, doctor?

Since you mention it, and since you are awake now, Rachel, I shall do so. Early on in Mr. Bettger's book, he makes a point that is as basic as gravity. It is the idea that your service is not and end in itself but is instead a means to the client's ends. He tells a story that I find instructive.

In the days of the Depression, the lot of an insurance salesman was indeed bleak. After a great deal of persistence he was
granted an interview with a modestly well-to-do businessman.
As he literally chased the businessman up and down the aisles
of his warehouse, he barraged the man with random questions
and finally, by good luck, struck oil. He had asked if the businessman had something in his life that he would like to have
continue after his own stroll through the Pearly Gates.

It turned out that the man had a son running a religious
mission in a remote part of the world. He wanted that son to
have continuous funding. After convincing the businessman
to buy the insurance, Bettger received such a large commis-
sion that he was asked to speak about the sale to other professional salespersons.

Here is where Bettger got his education about selling. After
the speech, Bettger was pulled aside and told by an experienced old salt that Bettger didn't understand what he had
done to achieve the sale. Of course Bettger protested that he
had just given a speech that gave chapter and verse about how
he had sold the businessman insurance. He was then reframed
nicely. The older salesman said that the client had a need to
fund his son. The businessman's need was for continuity not
for insurance. Bettger merely used insurance as a way to meet
that need.

There is a powerful message here. People don't need
NLPers, they need different results in their lives and NLPers
are one way to get those differences.

This means one thing in particular to a NLPer. You need to
be sure you have properly defined your product. Your product
is not NLPing. Our product is performance. The client wants
to think or feel differently so that he or she can get something
different than their current outcomes.

This also means that you are in competition against all of
the other possible means that the client has at hand, including
other professionals with different ways of attending to those
needs.

But, sir, how does that relate to selling as a professional NLPer?

I can think of a bunch of ways, Rachel. The first thing that comes to mind is the way you define your line of work. It is entirely too easy to burden yourself with the problem of doing things you don't believe in. For instance, if you service individuals only, you might want to enlarge your practice by seeking families to work with. But perhaps you know that you don't have fully developed behavioral models to do the best job on the complexities of family work. Your own lack of belief in the substance of your new product line will be evident in incongruities in your behavior and that will sabotage your most dedicated efforts. You won't be able to consistently close the sale since no one will believe in you. You could get by— maybe—but your own lack of belief in your skills will be evident. Don't you agree, Rachel? *Rachel??*

I think she's nodded off again, sir.

Or, (sigh) suppose you decide to forsake a private practice and pursue the big bucks that are rumored to be available in the world of business. But your information leads you to believe that big business is the kind of environment that is hostile to your caring, nurturing ways. After all, business is a competitive situation and you are convinced that competition means stress. If you have contempt or doubts about the value of the environment you are trying to work within, you are likely to come off as cynical and unbelievable.

You may get a bit of business here and there. But you won't do very well. The most successful people are those who believe in what they are doing.

In a comparable vein, you have to believe in your own specialty whether it is business consulting, therapy with anorexics, teaching, administration or whatever. For instance, if I were to write something about the cost effectiveness of owning a Rolls Royce, I strongly suspect readers would not buy it. That's because the point of owning a Rolls Royce, in my mind, is to prove that you are beyond the ordinary mortal concerns of what something costs. No matter how well I might do with the writing or the background research, my lack of conviction would somehow communicate itself to the audience.

Do you think that explains Rachel's fatigue, sir?

Benjamin!! Please!! No doubt the reader would sense that I was incongruent, i.e., speaking with a forked tongue. Someone else with less skill but more conviction would get the message across more effectively.

This brings us, handily, to another point I have noticed in the literature on selling. That is, the person needs to believe wholeheartedly in the product or service he is selling. Belief in the product definitely has an effect on others but it is also an attitude that has an effect on you. It pains me to say I have found a curious artifact of some NLPers' beliefs. It is this: Some NLPers believe in using the skills on their clients and customers in a formal work setting. Then, lo and behold, they indulge themselves emotionally because they do not think to use it on colleagues or their own family. (I won't get into the manipulation or spontaneity issues here.) They allow themselves to get angry at colleagues and family members over the same issues that get a different treatment if the other person is called a client.

If they don't get their way, they complain and blame and get upset . . . as though NLP is only for use on clients. Richard Bandler points out that none of us scold total strangers or clients. Why should one dispense with common courtesy and elicit negative responses from those we care about?

Is that why you aren't waking her up, sir?

(Hummppff) As for myself, I believe in NLP in this sense: If it works in one setting, it generalizes to other settings because NLP is about human nature no matter what setting or context we are considering. Such things as roles, goals, or contexts are arbitrary boundaries we think up to act as cues to set off appropriate responses.

But all of those items are subsets of human nature in general. Therefore, NLP is something you can believe in for virtually any human interaction. If you can't apply it in all contexts, it says more about your skills than anything else.

There is a relevant story that I ran across in another book on selling by Zig Ziglar. He makes the now-familiar point that a salesman needs to believe wholeheartedly in what he is selling.

One of Ziglar's friends was selling an expensive set of pots and pans for cooking and was not doing very well. After a bit of probing, Ziglar told the man he was not doing well because he didn't believe in the product. The man argued that he did indeed believe in the product as the most terrific thing on the market and blurted out his sales pitch about its merits. Ziglar, being observant, noticed the man did not have it on his own stove. So he asked: "If you believe in it, why aren't you using it yourself?" He got plenty of "reasons."

Now those of you who know me are aware that I have little use for "reasons." The salesman "justified" himself on the grounds that he had oodles of bills to pay, that the economy was down, and that as soon as he could afford it he would buy a set for himself.

This is a credibility issue, or an incongruity issue, if you like. Ziglar pointed out that customers gave the man the same excuse every day. How could the man tackle the objection when he believed it himself? Ziglar suggested that given the same situation, he'd mortgage his furniture to buy a set of the cookware he was selling. The man took his advice and the increase in his sales paid for the set in the first week.

Now how does all of that relate to NLPing? If NLP works on clients, it also will work on friends and family . . . if you use it. Try it. If necessary, pretend the other folks in your life are clients, too. Then you will have all-around success.

Sir? How would you sell Rachel on the value of a good night's sleep?

With difficulty, I assume. Which brings to mind another

instructive episode. Linda Sommer and I conducted an interview with a psychologist who wanted to work with us because she was impressed with our results. The psychologist's training was of the Freudian type of dynamic psychology. Even though I was originally trained in the same field, to my way of thinking, Freudian skills are antique. There are lots of antique collectors in the field but I am not inclined to be one of them.

I carefully informed her of my assessment of the limited value I sensed in her orientation. I didn't want to use her skills as they were formulated. After reassuring her this was not an oblique way to recruit her into one of our training programs, I made the point that what she was offering did not have a market in my territory.

I suppose that is a fancy way of saying I didn't want a Freudian on my staff. I'm sure there is still a small market for buggy whips as well as for some theories of psychology. I rejected her offer of assistance and I didn't plan to refer anyone to her either. She was persistent. She blamed me for being insensitive. (I seldom do that to a customer.) Eventually she got around to name-dropping and when that didn't work started to compare her credentials with mine.

Fortunately, I "outranked" her in the "establishment" credibility department. So she then blamed me for not being able to see through the credentials issue to her real "existential value" as a caring person. Since I couldn't buy even a cheap cup of coffee with such a phenomenon, I remained unpersuaded.

It sounds like she was as tough a case as Rachel, doesn't it?

Well, Benjamin, you should also know that the woman had knowledge of rapport skills and pacing and leading . . . and was doing none of it. She was arguing her point and we all know that no one wins an argument. Here comes the lesson of the day, class. Linda asked her why she wasn't using those skills to convince me. Her response was classic: "He's not a client. I don't need to do that stuff in REAL life with a colleague."

Ahhh. What a lesson I learned that day. Ahh, incongruity. Ahhh, credibility. I asked myself: How can a person be understanding in one situation and not in another? The psychologist only looked for needs to fill in the limited situation of the work setting. And we then had an explanation of her poorish ability to maintain a relationship with lovers and family. Change the context on her and it would elicit a very different attitude and a very different way of handling things. She really believed that her needs were paramount outside of the office and demanded that they be filled "because" of whatever rationale upon which she had based that presupposition.

Are there other ways we can find a need and fill it?

Yes, Benjamin. One of the reframes that I do with clients is called the Sales Reframe. It would have done some good for this psychologist, I think. Many of my clients and trainees have a very jaundiced attitude about selling as well as an intense negative reaction if it is suggested that they would do well to try a bit of selling in their work. That psychologist wasn't selling, she was demanding. Her model was credentials and self-worth and all sorts of other things. She didn't know people don't do things because of what she thinks they "ought to do."

People do things that make sense to them and if you can't find their needs and work from them you are going to be very handicapped, just like she was. To get others to think about this, I ask what selling means to them, and the answers range from sneaky coercion to unsavory and deliberate manipulation visited upon the hapless sellee.

Then I ask if they have ever explained something to another person. I lead them with suggestions such as convincing a childhood pal that the dive off the board into the pool is really fun and won't hurt. Or I might suggest that they describe a movie in glowing terms that launched the other person to the next showing. Or did they ever get a friend to change their brand of makeup after an effective description of the wonderfulness of the new brand? Somewhere in their history I will find examples of how they changed someone else's mind.

And that is what selling is all about. It is the art of changing another person's mind from what they are spontaneously thinking about an issue and then changing the way they think so that they actually do something different as a result. This means that the seller takes the responsibility for having been a cause in a series of cause and effect events that changed the other person in some observable way.

Many people are very reluctant to call themselves an agent of change or a cause of events. They feel it is manipulative. Paradoxically, many human-resource types in management call themselves change agents and don't know how to actually change behavior.

But think about what a therapist or NLPer or consultant does. The "expert" enters someone's personal space and works some verbal devices on the client and expects something to happen. But I find there are two schools of thought at this point. The wimps think that something mystical will happen inside the individual that is a function of unknown, invisible vapors that will unexplainably make the person change. They will take credit if the person gets better and will claim that it is the fault of the gods (or Freudian godlets like "resistance') if the person doesn't come around to the therapist's frame of wishful thinking.

The really good change agents will know when they are in over their heads and will only do things that they know or reasonably hope will have the particular effect they want.

A good practitioner is as deliberate in his or her moves as a brain surgeon. It is of limited value to be as vague as an Asian guru or a Rogerian therapist. Anyone who mixes up deliberate competency with unsavory manipulation is naive in the extreme.

Then, sir, do you mean that selling and therapy both involve the same deliberate intent as the persuasion involved in ro-mance?

How do you mean, Benjamin?

Well, when I'm out on a date, I sell my date on what I have in mind and try to convince her it will be as therapeutic for her as for me . . .

BENJAMIN!! I get the idea. Just wake up Rachel and we'll call it a day, okay?

You've sold me, sir.

CHAPTER FIVE

QUESTION POWER

Can you not think of a pink elephant? Of course you cannot . . . and the reason is that in nature a vacuum is instantly filled with air when there is even the tiniest leak. Nature abhors a vacuum. And the mind, when presented with the vacuum caused by a question, rushes to fill the vacuum with an answer. A person cannot NOT respond to a question. Try this exercise on your friends: Ask any questions such as "How are you?" or "What color are your mother's eyes?" or "What do you want for dinner?"

Even if the person does not want to answer you verbally, he or she will answer in their own mind . . . they have no choice. The uses of questions may be for presentations, speeches, casual conversation, courtroom arguments, sales, interviews, training, and more. The only requirement is two people or more. Thus a question has a very powerful effect. In fact, a question is the most powerful tool you have in interactions with others.

The Socratic Method

Socrates developed what may be the ultimate interview method about 450 B.C. His method is this: Ask a series of questions that will lead others to the conclusions that you want them to reach. This accurately implies that the other person in the dialog often does most of the talking. As a

QUESTIONER, Socrates would OBSERVE his subject's reaction and USE that reaction to decide what QUESTION to ask next. He repeated this series of steps (i.e., question, observe, use, question) until the subject reached the desired conclusion. Socrates rarely lost in selling his point of view. Nearly always, he changed the other's mind. The power of the question over the power of giving an opinion gave him the advantage.

Even though the Socratic method is yet to be outdone in the modern world, it has been enhanced in its effectiveness by the emergence of Neuro Linguistic Programming (NLP) as a means to refine the questioning even further than Socrates had managed to do with all of his sophistication. The objective, in any case, is to use questioning to change someone's mind. One aspect of NLP to consider is its systematic way of using the natural effects of language on thinking to CAUSE specific responses in the behavior of others.

NLP is a powerful vehicle of applying the Socratic method to the art of dialog in any form. NLP gives us a more refined sense of what to observe and how to use the information to sculpt the thoughts of another.

Opinions: Declarative or Interrogative

Opinions are like noses; everybody has one. But, if you offer your advice, it characteristically will elicit resistance, defensiveness, and various negative emotions. State an opinion if you must. However, test the difference in result when you end a simple declarative sentence with a TONAL QUESTION MARK on the last word or two. The reaction to a declarative sentence converted to an interrogative sentence with a tonal question mark at the end will be different.

Questioning requires a somewhat different skill than OPINIONATING or the DECLARATIVE STATEMENT approach to dialogue. The astute questioner must be prepared with

many modes or criteria relating to the process of human behavior (as well as the content of any given topical area such
as accounting, anatomy, sports, etc). Intelligent, leading, helpful questions can't be asked unless the questioner has a framework of mental maps to generate particular questions that
will produce results.

The process of questioning involves, at least partially, eliciting a response from someone and matching or comparing it to
some aspect of one's thinking models or mental maps to know
if the person has acquired the point at issue.

Questions and Criticism

Everyone is criticism phobic: At least it is helpful to assume
this. Questions have less chance of eliciting a criticism phobia
or POLARITY response (i.e., any negative emotion or response) and avoid dominance phenomena from taking charge
of dialog. If you inadvertently trigger off a phobic response by
criticizing someone, the resulting negative emotional response is so predominant that it is virtually impossible to then
get the message across that you originally intended. A question has a built-in foolproof character to it that virtually
makes criticism impossible . . . assuming that voice tones and
body language are congruent.

Rapport

The idea of rapport can be defined in many ways. For our
purposes, it means eliciting information from the other party
while maintaining (usually) the positive emotional states
needed to continue the dialog to its conclusion. There is no
more powerful tool available than the question to gain and
keep rapport. With comfortable voice tones and congruent
body language, the other person will typically fall into a grace-

ful pattern of exchange with the individual who guides the discussion with skillfully presented questions.

Pacing and Attention

An advantage to questioning is the reduced likelihood of overloading the person's ability to absorb and process the information generated. If the questioner goes too fast or too slow or is inattentive, the communication can come to nothing. An individual not skilled at observing cues that indicate an effective interpersonal exchange can easily run on with their verbalizations and not notice if the other person is lost, listening, daydreaming or in need of a restroom. When a question is asked there needs to be an attentive frame of mind to watch for the satisfactory response.

Of course there are horrible examples, such as Barbara Walters, who asks and answers her own questions in TV interviews. She pays little attention to the interviewee because she is attending to herself. If the verbal or non-verbal cues indicate a point has been missed, one does not as easily rush ahead of the subject's rate of response to your presentation. Pacing and attending to the audience is a basic prerequisite to an effective dialogue.

Participation

Besides the gains of effective pacing, questions elicit the participation of the other party to the dialog. A person will have difficulty being bored if asked questions relevant to his areas of interest.

The participation of the other is obviously but importantly a source of useful information. Voice, body language, eye movements, and many other response indicators of the communication's effectiveness are overtly displayed when the person's responses are elicited by well-formed questions. This means fine-tuned, calibrated questions need to be generated that will ultimately lead the person to the desired state and outcome that you and/or they have selected. Your abilities to refine their needs and desires automatically are increased by eliciting participation with questions and, of course, to repeat an earlier point, "Can you NOT think of a pink elephant?" The magic is that you have recaptured their mind with each step in the questioning sequence.

Time and Effort

Making a flat statement is easier to do and quicker than asking a question and waiting for a response. It would seem to be MORE EFFICIENT to tell someone the point to be made. But, is it MORE EFFECTIVE? Does telling get the outcome as surely as does questioning? Consider an example when the boss notices that the widgets are not completed:

A DIRECT APPROACH:
Boss:	You talk too much on the job.
Subordinate:	Oh yeah? Who says so?

AN INDIRECT APPROACH:
Boss:	Are you getting all the widgets done on time?
Subordinate:	Uh, well, almost.
Boss:	Is anything in particular slowing things down?
Subordinate:	I'll take a look at things to make sure we're done on time.

Of course this is a direct contrast between an unsuccessful argument-generating DIRECT approach compared to a positive response generated by an INDIRECT approach (i.e., questions). Indeed it is less efficient to question, but typically, it is more likely to get the effective outcome that is desired. It is rather like the difference of the Western movie fist-fight compared to the Eastern martial arts. Questions are more like Judo. They utilize the other person's own mental momentum to "throw" the problem without working up a sweat that comes from defining the dialog as a struggle.

Flat statements run at least a 50/50 chance of generating resistance because anyone's responses basically are either positive or negative to any given stimulus. Questions may need time and preparation to work, but they are comparatively effortless when matched to the alternative of forcing communications on others with blunt, direct approaches that generate resistance instead of cooperation. An interesting test is to spend a day ASKING half the time vs. TELLING during the other half of your dialogs. Keep score of the proportion of positive to negative reactions. It will be very enlightening.

Components

In essence, the Socratic method is simple: conduct a dialog with an individual or group by repeatedly ASKING QUESTIONS, OBSERVING responses, and UTILIZING the responses to lead the audience with more QUESTIONS to discover the answer or outcome. Important components of the process are as follows:

a. The other person has initially a PRESENT STATE of mind and the PAYOFFS that sustain that state of mind. Those payoffs must be utilized or displaced by other payoffs to CHANGE THE PERSON'S MIND. The dialog is the arena where this change takes place.

b. The DESIRED STATE or outcome that is wanted must be presupposed or defined, initially, to provide a tentative interview goal. The interview process is then used as the tool to produce the change of mind resulting in the desired outcome. It may be to sell a product, agree on a policy, negotiate a contract, produce a positive feeling and trust. The goal may be refined or changed many times in the course of the dialog as new information is elicited.

c. Question formulation is dependent on what the interviewer is able to observe and utilize, and those questions in turn are a function of the MENTAL MAPS or MODELS the interviewer knows. NLP has very useful models for mapping, eliciting, observing, and utilizing another's behavior. NLP is an especially powerful tool for eliciting useful information via questioning.

d. Observations can be useful even if one only has three useful categories to define audience responses which have been elicited (i.e., a POSITIVE, agreeing response; a NEUTRAL, indifferent response; a NEGATIVE, disagreeing response). Further refinements are possible and are treated elsewhere under the labels of Meta Model, The Yeager Performance Model, The Yeager Power Grid, Milton Model, and Metaphor Model. (See Dilts, et.al., 1980, and Yeager, et.al, 1982.)

.   UTILIZATION is what the interviewer does with the observed response elicited from the other person. Models of how to utilize are described in depth in the work of Bandler, Dilts, and others. Whatever the interviewee does is useful information. It is assumed that if the person is not cooperating or responding as desired, it is because the interviewer has not hit on the right combination of skills to elicit the proper response. If one assumes control of the interview, one also assumes the responsibility if it doesn't work. The interviewer must be flexible in his or her skills to make it work. As one of the sayings of NLP goes: "The way you holler at the mountain is the way your echo comes back." If you don't like the echo of your own stimulus, change the way you holler: do something else. Often, the other person's *choice of words* will *indicate* what you need to do to elicit their target response.

f. LEADING is simply the process of iteratively obtaining information that clarifies the present state and puts the implicit or explicit outcome that would define a successful conclusion. *The elicited information* shows the interviewer the way to *lead* the other person to the desired state or goal through the question, observe, utilize, and question sequence. Leading is the choice of methods used to steer the person to the desired outcome.

Models can be found in many forms—conceptual, theoretical, rules of thumb, guidelines, and so on. Language and math are perhaps the two most pervasive models for representing realities. *Models* are merely mental maps that help the individual *represent the territory of reality* as he has experienced it in his personal history. Models are necessary and natural and make it easier to traverse that territory. Modeling is an extensive subject and much can be learned from *Neuro Linguistic Programming, Vol. 1.* by Dilts, et.al. Many refinements in the general process of communication are possible. Perhaps the most elegant means available is via training in NLP. NLP is possibly the most useful technology available for utilizing the natural psychological effects of the Socratic method.

Interview Control: Competition vs. Cooperation

Many interviews are unnecessarily presupposed to be a struggle or competitive interaction. With effective interview control skills, the interviewer can assume and achieve a *cooperative* dialog and gain optimum results by avoiding argument and disagreement. As the Japanese have learned in business, *no one ever really wins an argument.* The interviewer has a built-in competitive advantage for his views, paradoxically, by conducting the interview as a cooperative process. He is also assumed to have REQUISITE VARIETY: the ability to respond effectively no matter what occurs. The person in the dialog with the most flexible repertoire of responses will prevail in determining the outcome.

It is useful to presuppose that *the other person wants something* that can be made relevant to the outcome the interviewer wants. *The interviewer must ask:* "How can I solve for his payoffs, and also get the payoffs I want?" A useful assumption to make is that in answering the following question you will know what payoffs to pursue for him to change his mind. The question is this: "HOW CAN I HELP YOU?" If you can *help the person obtain a payoff* relevant to themselves and in the process gain your own outcome then you've reached the ideal outcome of mutual gains.

There are many tools available to help one conceptualize the structure and functions of an interview. The Socratic method, extracted from the *Dialogues* using NLP techniques, seems to be virtually a universal approach. (There are other approaches, such as confrontational methods for instance.) Not the least among the advantages of the Socratic method is a positive emotional tone—one need never feel like a loser or feel put down. It is elegantly economical in the many aspects of human nature to which it harmoniously and comfortably adapts for enhancing human communication.

The Socratic method's structure is the refined use of questions, its *function* is to change another's mind. It allows a win-win vs. win-lose dialog.

Outcomes and the Dark Room Metaphor

A mistake the interviewer can make is to assume that the other's desired outcome is obvious from the start of the discussion. Without verifiable and sensory-based information of what the person wants, the interviewer is likely to be working on the wrong information and goals.

A likely gain as a result is to frustrate his own efforts with the Socratic model no matter how effective his use of it. It is very easy to solve the wrong problem without a clear, verified view of the goals the other has in mind.

One of the ways to resolve one's haste to closure is to think of a metaphor that effectively states the situation when an interview is initiated. Imagine that you have awakened after a terrific drunk in a totally dark room not knowing where you are or how you got there. What would you do? The typical answer is to carefully feel your way around until you know where the sharp objects are and can find a light or door without tripping over anything or falling down a flight of stairs. In a very real sense, when another person begins to talk to you, you are metaphorically in that dark room. You do not know, initially, what is on the other's mind with certainty, nor do you know where all the sharp objects are that you might bump into without some information.

It is clear then that the interviewer must spend a considerable effort in learning where the other's mind is in terms of goals, payoffs, resistance, and desired outcomes. That information must be elicited and melded with your own sense of mutual outcomes to make the whole process work.

Graphically summarized, the process can be represented by QOUQ to illustrate the steps for its mnemonic and strategic value in thinking. Any interview can be analyzed for its effectiveness by scoring for the repeated use of the process at each step or verbal statement of the interview. One must ask: "Is every statement in the interview actually one of the four steps in the QOUQ Model or has an interviewer slipped into declarative sentences or opinions statements of fact?" "Has the interviewer drifted into use of combative and argumentative tones instead of using the upturned voice tone at the end of a statement to turn it, at the very last moment, into a question instead of a challenge?" "Does the statement or opinion usually elicit a polarity response?" (i.e., a negative reaction).

Is the interviewer using the QOUQ sequence consistently and leading the person from the spontaneous frame of mind toward achieving the change of mind that is defined as the outcome or desired state? Take a sheet of paper and make a column of the letters:

QOUQ
QOUQ
QOUQ
QOUQ

repeatedly down the page and then analyze each utterance of the interviewer for his use of the model.

An example of how the Socratic method can be used follows in the sample dialog which follows. In this example, *Questioning* by "Joe Socrates" is obvious, as is *Utilization* of "O. Boy's" responses to go on to the next *Question*. Only the observation step is implied. At the end we see that "Joe Socrates" has *led* "O. Boy" skillfully, eliciting a positive response each time. He elicits no neutral or negative responses, and he succeeds in changing "O. Boy's" mind from a present state of mind that is ignorant and anxious to a state of mind that is informed and that will subsequently show in his behavior.

Joe Socrates wants to sell his office assistant, O. Boy, on a new word processing computer keyboard. The new keyboard will compute customer discounts in correspondence automatically rather than by hand calculation which is timeconsuming and awkward.

O. Boy hates to work with numbers, but has argued against the change due to anxiety that the next feature would be too hard to learn.

Socrates illustrates how easy and user-friendly the change can be. Especially notice how Socrates uses a clever selling method, as they sit at the word processor together.

SOCRATES: Do you notice, the keyboard has a separate set of keys to enter numerical information?

O. BOY: Yes, they are just off to the side of the regular keyboard.

SOCRATES: Does a move of your wrist easily position your hand over the numerical keyboard?

O. BOY: Yes, it does.

SOCRATES: Would you please touch the key marked "calculate" and enter this set of sample figures I'm handing you now?

O. BOY: O.K., here goes. (enters the numbers)

SOCRATES: Now that they are entered, would you touch the key marked "enter" and tell me what happens?

O. BOY: O.K. (pause) O, boy! It enters the figures in just the right place in the letter and the discount is already calculated.

SOCRATES: Does this eliminate several steps in producing correspondence?

O. BOY: Yes, it sure does.

SOCRATES: Is it easier to do the work this way?

O. BOY: Yes, it is.

SOCRATES: Do you prefer this new way over the old way?

O. BOY: Yes, of course. This is easy.

Thus the "Yeager QOUQ Model" is an effective representation of the Socratic method. Having the explicit strategy of Socrates available means we can see with X-ray eyes into words that look like ordinary dialog on the surface. Under the surface, now that we have a map at the appropriate chunk level (or level of detail), we can see how he did it and replicate the skills for ourselves. Such a time-proven tool can only be useful.

Clearly all of the components and criteria we have listed and discussed above have been recapitulated in this sort-of Socratic dialog. He posed questions that led O. Boy, observed the response, and utilized the information to lead to the next step until O. Boy reached the desired conclusion.

The question for you now is: "When can you demonstrate your new skills at questioning?"

References

Dilts, R. et. al., *Neuro Linguistic Programming Vol. 1*

CHAPTER SIX

THOUGHTS ON A REFRAME

A reframe is a curious creature. It uses verbal or nonverbal language to change the meaning of something. There is a comment going around in the circles of cognitive psychologists that says: "It is not the events in themselves that upset us but rather our interpretation of the meaning of the events that determines our response." That was said by Marcus Aurelius, the ancient leader.

In a condensed form it means that we learn to think of an event as good, bad, likeable or not, positive or negative, and so on. It may even be that we have an instinct to respond to things with like, dislike or neutrality. After all, what other possibilities are there? But how that instinct is used is a matter of individual learning. For example, in modern culture, incest is frowned upon, while in ancient Egypt it was standard practice. One hundred years ago, ". . . a glimpse of stocking was looked on as something shocking," but now, ". . . heaven knows, anything goes." Study your average issue of *Vogue* or *Penthouse* and you will see a lot more than a glimpse of stocking.

Since there is no "instinct" for telling us the intrinsic meaning of things, we must learn what things around us mean. The most adaptable of us are those who have the ability to learn all the most important meanings of any given event. I call it the multiple choice of behavior which is applied to all the coping and adaptive events we must encounter in a life span.

Reframing techniques are a means of taking a more or less singular interpretation of an event and giving it new or different or multiple meanings. The result of course is that the "knower" of this multi-faceted meaning will have variable as opposed to rigid responses due to increased discrimination power to make distinctions that gives the person the choice of how to respond according to the learned meaning that he or she has acquired.

Reframing techniques provide substantial leverage for change. Reframes essentially rearrange thought patterns and components so that a stimulus takes on multiple meanings instead of limited meanings. This results in the person having a choice of responses when presented with the stimulus. For example, in selling, a customer may complain that the price is too high. A successful reframe would convince the customer that the high price is an indication of the quality that is needed to insure durability or whatever.

In the following discussion, I thought you'd like to know how the "competitive" reframe of Yeager and the "universal" reframes of Sommer came about and are useful to a practitioner.

Although the early book *Frogs Into Princes* by Bandler and Grinder describes the six-step reframe in early and successful form, the basic reframe has undergone many transformations.

For example, I was able to change the six-step into a one-step. I was sitting with a client and told her this: "You know, Erickson had the notion that there are two people in the same sack of skin. The unconscious and the conscious person. He also found out that you can have a conversation with both of them. For instance, did you notice your toes until I just pointed them out to you?" (The answer is always no. Pick any body part you like as long as you can factor it into the discussion congruently.)

"Well, the fact is that your unconscious mind was aware of that and its job is to take care of things that you have learned so your conscious mind can rely on automatically generated behavior by the unconscious. You don't necessarily want to be aware of each behavior, you want the results you want.

For example, in most cases you don't want a car as much as you want to be at your destination. A car is just a means to get somewhere. What you learn is often not an end in itself. Instead, any given learning is useful as a means to achieve some other end. In a similar fashion, our unconscious mind takes care of the things you don't have time to be bothered with in a conscious way." And, this continues. . . .

"I bet you'd be surprised to know that your unconscious mind is listening to me right now and if I ask it to talk to us, you will find it is very cooperative and it will answer. You may not be at all aware of the way the unconscious communicates." At times I will not tell them the signal or ask them to even try to elicit their own signal. I will just call it forth and congruently talk to the part while the client sits there in amazement as I have a conversation with an invisible person. I will say something to the part like: "Since you have been listening to this, I presume you are ready to communicate." I then watch for an external response to that question. As it occurs, I will thank the part.

I will then proceed: "The neat thing is that this discovery wasn't made until just a couple of years ago. In fact your unconscious is listening to me right now. If I ask the unconscious a question, how would you, the conscious person, like to sit back and notice what goes on? O.K. unconscious part, I know you are helping her." I presupposed that idea in a set-up that defines symptoms as *friends* and as emotional radar and that symptoms are telling you to do something different.

By analogy, a ship's captain would turn on his radar and know if he was headed for the rocks. If so, he'd know to turn the boat. An uncomfortable feeling has the same role. It tells you to change what you are doing. All we have to do is ask it what it needs you to do differently to achieve your preferred results. Once you communicate with the unconscious, you will have its help in making sure you are able to get what you want and need.

"Does she (or he) need to do 'X'?" Selecting the topic for "X" has been supplied by the nominalizations and needs already defined by the client in the elicitation phase. You *echo* those words back to the client at this point. There is ALWAYS a signal from the unconscious. Sometimes I ask the part to amplify the signal so the conscious mind knows it, too. At other times it is nice to leave the conscious person in a perplexed state while I tell them to just sit there as I talk to the part and they are kind of amazed at this weird dialog I am having that they can't figure out. I decide to use this tactic mostly on the basis of the presence of a strong client polarity response.

A polarity responder can't get a word in edgewise against themselves when they are the one who is actually doing the talking! So I elicit from the unconscious the need and the prescription and the agreement of the part to insure that the behaviors will be available on cue and ask other questions about when and how the client will become aware of the changes to keep their conscious mind from becoming impatient if the process needs a little time.

Now, let's proceed with more thoughts on reframes.

Recipes for Reframes

Using a six-step reframe on one particular client produced some unusually pervasive and powerful results by combining it with a sports-oriented metaphor. Curiosity led to testing the way the reframe was done on others and the results seem to generalize to other clients. The way the reframe was done and some thoughts about what may be going on are offered here as a resource for other practitioners.

Painting with broad brush, the 35-year-old woman executive was concerned about not being in control of many on-the-job factors that were affecting her mood, productivity and personal life. The presenting state was a sense of helplessness, depression, and the symptoms of what is commonly called job-burnout syndrome. Her desired state was to be able to influence the people in her working environment to her satisfaction, and to get her career moving. She was with a manufacturing firm and had been previously treated by several psychiatrists for depression.

In eliciting her concerns and strategies, a metaphor involving sports (football) was employed to clarify her present and desired states at a rather large chunk level. As she listed her behaviors and limitations involving the depression, they were characterized at a similar large chunk level with comments such as "Oh, you *lost* on that play" or "You feel you didn't *win* (or *score*) on that play." Other items elicited referred to her "game plan and game strategy" (which was to not lose her job and to make her career progress).

It was also elicited and characterized that she was mostly on the *defensive* in interactions with others, seldom gained any yardage and had not taken the offensive when occasions called for initiative. Most of her behaviors were characterized as to whether they helped her score and win. She also decided that she wanted as a desired state to increase her ratio of wins in work and personal situations and that it would require that she be interpersonally more assertive rather than as passive, angry, and withdrawn as she tended to be.

She was also presented with the notion, through a verbal reframe, that her job situation was actually more *competitive* rather than *social* in its nature. This helped her distinguish the competitive from social interactions. She realized she would need to be more competitive in her desired outcomes. This sports metaphor set the stage for deciding which "parts" would be elicited during the six-step reframe.

The parts elicited were the *"game planning"* part (variously labeled when used at other times the strategy part, the planning part, the winning-losing part, or the offensive-defensive part). The *creative* part was elicited to figure out the many *moves* or *plays* (behavioral choices) that the person had in repertoire. The game planning part was instructed to use the more varied assertive plays.

The strategy part acknowledged its score-keeping function and was instructed to reward the person with a sense of accomplishment every time there would be a score. Winning was defined partially as being in the interpersonal and career game of choice and as making gainful moves on the job and socially.

A third useful part elicited was the "happy" part which allowed the person to *enjoy* all the changes as they would come about. This is a fun way of putting icing on the cake.

The client reported after the reframe that her entire life was changing and that all of her relationships were improved, that she was very much in control of her job situation, and that her job-burnout symptoms had disappeared. She was taking the offensive and was winning and getting the results she wanted most of the time rather than rarely. Her assertive and persuasive skills were in full flower and she was very pleased.

Her ratio of wins to losses went up dramatically. She had taken charge of her life. She spent no more time being naively idealistic, wishing that the rules of the game would be changed to be less competitive.

To generalize from this case to others, many clients have a basic pattern of interpersonal coping or problem solving that can be described as dependent and defensive in nature as opposed to offensive. They do not display a variety of responses to fit their circumstances and that results in their losing more than they win in life situations. The sports metaphor seems to work well as a highly leveraged reframe that has the potential to modify an even wider-than-usual range of client responses. Its potential pervasiveness might be compared to the Transactional Analysis idea of a "Life Script." In the hierarchy of response chunks this interpersonal area seems to be a large and pervasive one.

Experience with other clients has validated that preliminary to the six-step reframe, reference to the sports metaphor sets the stage nicely to help adjust their responsiveness to the idea that they are often in competitive situations that they have not recognized and the new ways of responding are useful to have.

Taking football as a point of reference is arbitrary. Many

other sports may work as well. But using football makes it easy to characterize a client's behavior in terms that are easily related to most people's models. It is also useful to formulate questions about their strategies and to communicate metaphorically about the type of useless loops they may be processing. For example:

— Is the client primarily too defensive and passive or too offensive and aggressive to achieve desired outcomes?

— Does the client confuse being in the action with scoring, i.e., are there "self-awareness" loops with no exit?

— Does the client have an offensive strategy that works in a variety of interpersonal situations, such as being persuasive and oblique as well as being direct, blunt, and forceful?

— Does the client lose ground or merely hold ground and confuse that with scoring?

— Does the client engage in the same action play after play and not reach the goal or outcome?

— Does the client not recognize the differences among playing, scoring, and winning?

— Does the client have many resource plays (e.g., assertive, passive, aggressive) that will cover a variety of situations?

Another way of looking at it is in terms of the recent stress literature. Do they have *fight* as well as *flight* responses when they want them? At least two other situations described below have come to mind to illustrate other applications of the sports metaphor about winning and losing as prelude to a reframe. The common feature of those observed is that they have not exited from a large-chunk TOTE. They get very few of the outcomes they want in many life encounters.

First, practitioners of conventional dynamic therapies work with a system that is heavy on diagnosis and light on prescription. The most frequent prescriptions that are offered are loops back to more refined diagnoses and "insight" and "awareness" because their system has no exit via a technology of behavior change. They often confuse talking about cure with the cure, they use the same plays over and over again, gain no yardage, can't tell that they are not scoring and blame the client if they don't win. Superstitious learning abounds when by a lucky accidental verbal reframe, for instance, a client improves and they feel they have validated their losing, no-exit, no-win system.

Second, religious systems and astrology share this problem at times. One client was observed who had a very well developed Sufi religious rationale. Much of the content of the system was elegantly metaphorical of strategies such as creativity, learning, etc., and many desirable outcome states were defined as chakras, inner light, be calm, be peaceful, be at one with God, etc. The limitation the client experienced was that the labeling of the inner resources defined by the religious system did not permit the client to win in any useful way. The chunk level was too large and it tends to be past-not present-oriented, too.

Also, most of the states and strategies elicited by the system were intended to be used by the person to overcome problems produced by insufficient, competitive human relationship skills that were obscured by the content of the system. As a no-exit system, the Sufi rationale defined virtually all of life's human problems in terms that did not serve this individual to generate behavioral flexibility because of the large and useless chunk level. As a result, the person's primary response to most strategies was to loop into downtime called "self-awareness." However, these types of religious metaphors would seem to be potentially useful if they could be chunked down into strategy steps.

In both these examples, i.e., dynamic therapy and a religious system, the persons using the system operate it like a macro-level TOTE with no exit. In terms of the sports metaphor, the client cannot win with such a pattern since there is no exit. Of course, responses other than a reframe might be useful for clients, but let's return to the reframe for now.

This verbal reframe via sports metaphor precedes the six-step reframe rationale and applies very well to those situations where the person is not especially effective at assertive skills. A common observation made (and fixable via a verbal reframe) is that people often do not make a clear distinction between interpersonal situations that are *social* as opposed to *competitive.* Working a social model in a competitive situation is defeating.

A difference might be, for example, the school dance as opposed to a school football game. The football game is defined as competitive and calls for competitive skills. Most people are more likely to define the school dance as social and non-competitive (although there are exceptions who define virtually everything as competitive). Using a social model in a competitive context (especially a corporate job context) is a sure cause of problems. Most job situations are competitive and it is amazing how many people do not recognize this fact.

Once the context has been marked out with the verbal reframe as the competitive situations versus social, the sports metaphor frame of reference is useful to then characterize the specific behaviors the client offers as either offensive or defensive, as winning or losing in nature, as following a strategic game plan or random in nature, as gaining or losing yardage, or as scoring or just going back and forth on the field of play, or as having a flexible repertoire of plays and interpersonal tactics so they can win (and to make sure they don't give back points they've won as some clients do).

These game plan behaviors are quite pervasive and the changes based on this frame of reference seem to have wide-ranging impact.

We now come to a very interesting issue developed by Linda Sommer, Co-director of the Eastern NLP Institute. She has identified some very important adaptive behavior patterns that people use to defend themselves. The patterns are so pervasive that they have been dubbed "universal" in their impact.

Sommer's Universal Reframes

A Universal Reframe is a reframe on a pattern that is part of our behavior. For example: We protected ourselves as children with common behaviors such as crying, running home, hiding, fighting, getting help from our older brother or sister, etc. As adults we modify the externals of the experience by sarcasm, hibernation, shyness, arguing, etc.

The way that the Universal Reframe works is this. It is presupposed that the intention of the behavior is positive. All we want to do is update the way in which we are protected so that it matches or is appropriate to where we are now (today). We ask the protective part to come up with new ways of protecting us that are more appropriate for now.

Procedure:

_____ 1. **PRACTITIONER SAYS:** Choose a tone that would be befitting for such a powerful part. Ask the protective part if it would please communicate with you in consciousness. Be aware of anything you see, hear, or feel. Sometimes it is manifested in breathing changes, eye blinks, burps, so pay close attention to everything.

(Watch minimal cues.) If they say, "I think I got a signal, but I'm not sure," thank that part very much and ask it, if indeed that was the signal would it please intensify? Thank the part very much.

_____ 2. **CLIENT SAYS:** (You can do this aloud for the client, if you like). I'd like to thank you for being there for me all this time. You've been doing a great job because I am alive and well. However, I am not the same person I was 10 years ago, a year ago, a week ago or even a day ago. What we would like to do is update the way you protect me so that I will know I am protected in a way that is more appropriate to where I am now. Would you assist me (person's name) in creating new behaviors or ways of protecting me that are more appropriate for me now? Thank you very much.

OPTIONAL-I will tell the client that the part already knows what is needed. It was waiting for them to ask for the assistance.

_____ 3. **CLIENT ASKS:** Protective part, do you know what I need to be protected more appropriately for where I am now? Thank you very much.

_____ 4. **PRACTITIONER SAYS:** I'm going to invite one more part in. Your FUN part. We want to make sure that being protected is fun and the new behaviors will be enjoyable in creating and utilizing them.

_____ 5. **CLIENT ASKS:** (Choose a tone that would be appropriate for the fun part - tones are anchors.) FUN part, will you please communicate with me in consciousness? (You can embed it to respond with a smile or something similar.)

Once you get your signal, tell it what you are doing. Ask if it would be kind enough to assist the protective part in coming up with new ways to protect you, to ensure that the process will feel good along with the new behaviors. Thank it very much.

_____ 6. **PRACTITIONER SAYS:** Now I will give the directions to both parts. I invite your conscious mind to do whatever it wants to while I talk to the unconscious. I respectfully request that you keep the new behaviors out of the conscious awareness of _____ so that they can be pleasantly surprised as the new behaviors are manifested. If however, you think it is important to show them one or two, please do. Rather than having expectations we would like to have pleasant surprises.

Instructions to the Protective Part and the Fun Part

PRACTITIONER SAYS: Thank you again for being willing to assist _____ in coming up with new behaviors and ways of protecting themselves in more appropriate ways. This is the way I would like you to proceed. First make a picture of the new behavior, keeping that image out of the conscious awareness of _____. Decide whether it is in color, or black and white, a movie or a still, focused, or defocused, the appropriate brightness for you, the right size of the picture, the distance in front of you that is appropriate.

Do all of the components of the visual system. When you are completely and fully satisfied with what you see, go on to the auditory components. Decide on the right volume for the new behaviors, pitch, tone, intonation, accent, rate of speech, rhythm - all of the component parts of the sound system.

When you are completely satisfied with what you see and what you hear, STEP INTO the picture. If it feels great, thank the parts very much and proceed to the next behavior. If, however, it needs any adjustments, step out of the picture, make the necessary adjustments just as you would for a computer or a TV set, and step into it again. When you are COMPLETELY satisfied with the way it looks, sounds, and feels, say thank you and move on the next behavior.

Do this for at least five new behaviors or as many as is appropriate. (Your part knows how many it needs or wants.) Remember to have a good time!!! Please signal us when you are through (perhaps a smile). Something big!!

_____ 7. While their unconscious mind is working I will often read or tell a metaphor that is isomorphic and related to what the protective part does. Words in stories are easily changed so that you can play with tenses, names, embedded commands, etc.

_____ 8. When they get their signal that they are through, check it yourself. Very often they are trying to consciously have control. While the parts are working or when they are finished ASK: Protective part, are you still working? Or are you finished working? Calibrate for the minimal cues. If you are satisfied that the work is done, thank the parts individually very much. If, however, you notice that the part is going to work for a long time, you have this option:

OPTION: Say: Protective and fun part, we're very pleased that you are coming up with so many new behaviors. If we show you how to complete this exercise, would you be willing to complete it the same way when you have finished generating behaviors? (Calibrate.) Thank you very much.

_____ 9. **PRACTITIONER SAYS:** THANK the fun part for assisting and thank the protective part for being willing to come up with these new behaviors to assist you in achieving that which you want to achieve in ways that are useful and appropriate for you.

_____ 10. **PRACTITIONER ASKS:** Are there any other parts that want to contribute to or be included in the new behaviors? Wait for a signal. If there is a signal, presuppose that the part really just wants to be included.

PRACTITIONER SAYS: Thank you very much for letting us know you are there. You are going to be affected by these new behaviors and we're pleased that you want to know what is going on and how you will be affected. Thank you for wanting to be informed and taking the responsibility in wanting to know what is going on.

PRACTITIONER ASKS: "Protective part and the fun part, please invite this new part in and give it an update (or overview) of all the new behaviors you have come up with." If the new part wants to add things please invite it to do so, and to be a part of all future changes. Have the parts do this briefly. Check to see if this new part is satisfied (it usually is). Thank it very much for caring enough to be included. Let it know it is appreciated.

____ 11. **CELEBRATE!!!** Have all of the parts celebrate the good job they did. Have them signal you when they are partied out.

____ 12. **PRACTITIONER ASKS:** "Protective part, will you take the responsibility to manifest at least some of the new behaviors between now and the next two weeks so _____ will know just how protected they are? Thank you very much." (Sometimes you might have to suggest a different time frame. The part will let you know.)

____ 13. **PRACTITIONER SAYS:** Parts never make an agreement unless they are willing to keep their word. So you will be in for many pleasant surprises in the next few weeks as new behaviors that are also fun will manifest for you.

____ 14. **CLOSE THE EXERCISE WITH A VISUAL SQUASH**

Take one hand and title it	— The protective part is in this hand
Take the other hand	— The fun part is in this hand
In middle	— The parts that asked to be included are in the middle of both

SLOWLY bring the two hands together and integrate the fingers. Then have them bring their hands flattened and together into their heart space. Instruct them to take five deep breaths.

PRACTITIONER SAYS: "Your parts do really great work for you. As you continue to breathe slowly it's wonderful to know that your parts are there for you, the entire person. They each have their own task, however. Their main function

is to assist you, _____ , the entire person, to achieve
what you need and want in ways that feel good and are comfortable. With each breath you take as you begin to come back
now you'll really feel good knowing how willing your parts are
to work with you for you. It is really something to feel good
about. You will be very pleasantly surprised to discover the
new ways you are protected and the fun you'll have feeling
protected. You do great work!! CONGRATULATIONS!!"

Metaphor for Use With Reframe

The following metaphor is used during step seven The specific metaphor used is adapted from the storybook, *The Dream
Tree,* by Stephen Cosgrove. You can purchase this book
through the Institute. Please note that there are many Milton
model patterns used in this story (which is our own adapted
version). A tape of this procedure and metaphor are available
upon request for a nominal fee. Use your knowledge of submodalities especially auditory components, matching and pacing techniques skillfully to elicit the response you want.

Coding: _____	=	name
(dark small print)	=	instruction of some sort
ALL CAPS	=	important embedded command. Emphasize the words subtly
underlined word	=	special emphasis (follow notated instruction)

There are many more embedded commands and Milton patterns that are in the story and many I'm sure you will want
to add. Auditory submodality components are very important
in doing this metaphor. Make sure you know what the desired
state is and then use this and vary accordingly.

Delivery is what makes sense of your words to the unconscious. Make sure your delivery matches your intentions.

Practitioner says: I'm going to tell you a story in about 30 seconds to keep your conscious mind occupied while your unconscious mind does its work. The name of this story, believe it or not is called _____ **(their name)** Caterpillar. Oh yes. Well, this caterpillar is a very curious caterpillar. She (he) loves to wriggle and giggle her way through the leaves and grass because it always tickles her tummy.

One day while she was wriggling and giggling her way through the grass and leaves she came upon a perfectly formed white cocoon. She had never seen one before and decided to go home and ask her friend **(could be a teacher, friend, wizard, etc.)** what it was. She sat on the toadstool couch and said to her friend, "Friend, what is a cocoon?" Her friend smiled and said, "You know _____ Caterpillar, one day SOON when we grow just a little more, you and I are going to build ourselves a cocoon, and **(set up)** then YOU _will_ **(say "will" so it can hardly be heard)** GO INSIDE and there you _will_ **(say "will" so it can hardly be heard)** dream the dreams of the dream tree. It is safe, comfortable, sooo protected."

(Here you will put in whatever information is relevant to the desired outcome of the client. For example, with a client who is ineffective in interpersonal relationships and experiences fear often, you may briefly describe dreams in which the client experiences the use of resources such as self-confidence, asking for what they want, asking for clarification rather than mindreading, enjoying feelings of satisfaction, of being protected and safe in appropriate ways.)

"It is here that all you wish to achieve in the ways that are appropriate and useful for you will come to pass in a way that feels sooo good, etc. And when you emerge," said her friend, "you _will_ **(say "will" so it can hardly be heard)** BE TRANSFORMED into a BEAUTIFUL butterfly."

"Well," _____ Caterpillar thought, "that was one of the

silliest things I've ever heard." She looked at her body and couldn't imagine how this furry, crawling caterpillar could BE TRANSFORMED into such a beautiful butterfly. Her friend just smiled at her and said, "Someday you'll know little caterpillar. Someday, _you'll_ **(emphasize the YOU in a higher ascending pitch and make the LL hardly pronounceable) know."**

Being as curious as she was _____ Caterpillar decided to find herself a butterfly and ask what it was like. So she wriggled and giggled her way through the forest, because it tickled her tummy, and found a special spot near a tree, and waited for a butterfly to come by. After a while a butterfly came by and _____ Caterpillar asked, "Mr. Butterfly, Mr. Butterfly, what does it feel like to be a butterfly?" The butterfly looked down and smiled, and then flew away. Well, _____ Caterpillar didn't like THAT response one little bit, so she decided (because she knows what she wants to know) to wait and ask another butterfly.

Soon enough another butterfly came by and she asked, "Mr. Butterfly, Mr. Butterfly, PLEASE tell me what it's like to be a butterfly." The butterfly looked down and smiled and said, **(use the same tonality as before)** "Someday you'll know, little caterpillar, someday you'll know." Well, _____ Caterpillar did receive an answer, however, it wasn't exactly what she wanted, so she thought and thought. Aha, she said, "I know what I'll do. When it is MY turn to become a butterfly, I'll come back and tell ALL of my caterpillar friends what it feels like to be a butterfly." And having resolved that dilemma, _____ Caterpillar felt good, and decided to play. So for the next 10–14 days she played and had a wonderful time. It FEELS SOOO GOOD to HAVE SOOO MUCH FUN.

Well, one day her antennae began to quiver and shake, and she knew that NOW IT IS TIME TO GO INSIDE AND BUILD YOUR COCOON. So she GOES INSIDE and builds your cocoon. There she dreams the dreams of the dream tree. All of the transformations that you'd like to have in ways that are appropriate for you take place in ways that are comfortable and useful. (**Laundry list the desired outcome in embedded commands. This is the time you install the desired outcome with ease.**)

And so she dreamed the dreams of the dream tree and probably tonight and for the next few nights you'll dream your own dreams in your dream tree that will integrate and be there for you, that FEELS SO GOOD, SO PLEASANT.

About 10 days to two weeks later first one wing emerged and then the other wing slowly emerged. _____ came out slowly and knew that she felt different ALL OVER and she knew that NOW she IS TRANSFORMED into a BEAUTIFUL butterfly. She went to the edge of the branch on the most beautiful tree and waited for a passing breeze. She waited and soon a breeze came by and MAJESTICALLY lifted her up in the air. She felt so free. She feels the breeze under her wings, and FEELS SO SAFE, SO FREE, SO COMFORTABLE, so (**add here whatever additional embedded suggestions that are appropriate**) that she decided to just HAVE FUN AND FEEL GREAT.

She thought of her friends and the promise she made about going back to tell them, but she FEELS SO GREATthat she decided to stay and float free, and comfortable and ENJOY all the new FREEDOM and LIGHTNESS and COMFORT that she now has available to her. So she floated majestically in the air, gently floating as the breezes lift her high as she ELEGANTLY, and EASILY, ENJOYS the feelings she is now having.

Far below, ____ Butterfly heard a voice. She looked down and heard a little caterpillar say, "Ms. Butterfly, Ms. Butterfly, what does it feel like to be a butterfly?" And ____ Butterfly knew what her answer had to be. She looked down at the tiny caterpillar, and smiled, and said, "Someday you'll know little caterpillar, someday you'll know (**using same tones as earlier**).

Without pausing for more than five seconds ask the protective part if it is still working. Wait for the response and continue with the next step. That, essentially, means wrapping up the session with your usual closing devices.

There are variations that are indicated by these following criteria. The Protective Reframe is indicated when:
— Client feels uncomfortable about wanting help, or feeling vulnerable, or nervous about the session
— Client is scared (in their model) of whatever
— Client has nervous energy
— Client is afraid to speak up for themselves
— Client is angry, shy, mean or has a facade
— Client has any phobias, traumas, etc.
— Client wants to feel in control and safe
— Client that is associated and sorts emotionally most of the time
— Client that demonstrates an incongruity between internal and external states or fourtuples

All across the board this is a reframe that is useful without having to have specific indicators. Since it is so personalized, it means something different to each person. Can you think of anybody who wouldn't want to feel safer, or more protected about something in their life? In some context?

Another reframe is the "Attending To" Reframe. Again this is a universal reframe which means that it is universally a desirable reframe. Some indicators are:
— Client that always needs approval from an external source
— Client that is not taking good personal care of themselves
— Client that has any conflict that relates to external approval or imprints
— Client that has a difficult time making decisions if somebody else is involved or because of the above
— Client that gets their K+ externally
— Client that has a A i/d and then a K-i

— Client that feels somehow they have been denied something (feeling gypped)

— Client that is afraid to be good to themselves or denies themselves "little" pleasures or scores only losses compared to an impossible ideal

— Client that sorts good/bad comparison and usually doesn't measure up to their idea of good or doesn't compare well to others

By using the embedded command that the unconscious knows what a person needs in order to better attend to their own needs, it really doesn't matter what indicator there is. You cannot find me someone who doesn't want to somehow attend to what will make them feel better or have their life work better or be happy in a comfortable and balanced way, without having to be personally involved in the conscious decision.

Summary

The notion of the reframe is a pervasive NLP idea. The meaning of virtually any idea or feeling can be changed for added benefit to the individual. The added meaning implies an expanded behavioral repertoire and thus more free choice for the person. And that is a great deal of what NLP is about—choice.

CHAPTER SEVEN

ON MIND READING: HOW NOT TO DO IT

Good morning ladies and gentlemen.

Good morning, sir.

For today's topic, I'd like to cover an item that is a building block of our "cognitive construction" known as NLP. Of course, those of us in the know subscribe to the notion (except when we don't) that reality is constructed in the mind. If it is helpful, reality is *learned* for homo sapiens, it is not instinctive. Doesn't that sound exciting, class?

That sounds very exciting, sir.

Michael, your note of sarcasm hasn't escaped my keen observation skills. Does that mean that you are well versed on the subject and ready to assist me in this discussion?

Quite the contrary, sir. Why, just the other day at a Woody Allen film festival, I was discussing the problem of determining how we know what we know. It's a very big subject and even Woody Allen conceded the difficulty of knowing if there is an Intelligence in the Universe, even if one excludes certain parts of New Jersey.

Indeed, Michael. However, your cosmic-intelligence perspective is a little global. We will find it simpler to deal with one or two ways that we manage to confuse ourselves via our internally constructed reality . . . especially when it doesn't quite match up with external reality. An example of this is a story I heard about a "sky diver" who had utter confidence in the safety of his hobby. A friend asked how the diver could be so convinced of it's safety. The diver answered with perfect assurance this way: *When you leave the airplane you pull the rip cord for the first parachute. If it doesn't open, don't worry, you have plenty of time to open the second chute. If it doesn't open by that time, you are only about ten feet from the ground and any fool can jump ten feet!*

It is an interesting version of reality. One of the ways many of us construct similar illogical or unreal realities in our minds is through "mind reading."

What do you mean by "mind reading," sir?

I was just about to tell you, Rachel. But since you asked, turnabout is fair play because I notice you do it quite often, Rachel. Mind reading is the bad habit of jumping to a conclusion when you have no business doing so. Since, in mind reading, you act on something that doesn't exist, yet seems real, it is fiction. You are then living a soap opera, not real life.

Really sir! I think you are trying to turn me into a bad example in front of the class to embarrass me!

Ah . . . perfect, Rachel. You have just made my point for me. Well class, did any of you notice what just happened? Michael?

I don't think there is any way she could be sure about your intention, sir. Is that what you mean?

Yes, Michael, that is exactly what I mean. My motive was rather vague if you consider the evidence. How could Rachel know my intention? The answer is that she couldn't know it unless she pried some more information out of me. Instead she jumped to the conclusion that I was trying to embarrass her. That tendency to compare a situation to one's own frame of reference instead of that of the speaker is a very common way to write fiction. That is, Rachel responded on the basis of "make believe" information rather than on verifiable facts. Rachel, did you notice that you felt very certain of your conclusion?

Well, I still feel I was right because here you go again, sir, trying to embarrass me with more questions.

Aha! There you have it, class! She "feels" she is right. And that is the point. There are many times when we are seduced by the feeling of certainty. It is one of the limiting features of the psyche that it "convinces" us we are right and the convincer is the FEELING itself. There are many "feeling junkies," as I call those who are seduced by the certainty of that feeling. They go to great lengths to engineer situations so they can have that feeling . . . often by "putting down" another person. That kind of feeling is at the root of most prejudice.

If you would consider for a moment the fact that many mental strategies have as their last step a kinesthetic component. That "feeling" makes us feel we are finished with the thought and lets us proceed to the next thought. . . . even if the feeling is premature in terms of valid information.

No doubt Hitler felt he was right when he thought up the "final solution." Such a feeling tends to preclude the ability to think a competing or alternative thought which might be more accurate. And remember, our task in NLP is to add choices to our clients' behavioral repertoire.

When a scientist "mind reads" nature, the usual result is a failed experiment. As a result scientists tend to gather facts, evidence, data and information. If someone asserts that the moon is made of green cheese, the scientist will admit he or she doesn't know what it is made of and will try to find out by gathering facts in some systematic way so the facts can be tested. In the interpersonal sphere, people "feel" they are entitled to opinions. Often that means they have the luxury of acting on phony facts without bothering to check them out. Such an approach is the source of many arguments.

Well, sir, I think it is wrong of you to accuse me of starting an argument.

I'm not sure I agree with your assessment of my intention, Rachel. Perhaps I can persuade you with another line of thought. Mind reading is, in one sense, a case of lousy, choiceless logic. If you'll notice, there are several possible intentions I may have in mind such as making a point, utilizing a spontaneous classroom situation, soliciting a real-life example, and so on.

So in this example, you would be rolling the dice against poor odds if you were to conclude I was doing any of those without more reliable information. The problem with the feeling of certainty is that it can be very deceiving. It is the basis for much prejudice and that word "prejudice" literally means to "prejudge" something before the facts are in. A Ku Klux Klansman feels he is superior to non-Klansmen. That feeling doesn't necessarily make it true from the perspective of those who use other measures and criteria that are different than feeling.

If you are unfortunate enough to act on the basis of mind reading you will likely be wrong more often than you will be right just on the basis of the odds. In any given situation, there are several optional ways to interpret it. If there are several ways and you are "guessing" outcomes by virtue of mind reading, your odds are only that fraction represented by the one choice you make out of all the possible alternatives. If there are four options then your odds of being right are only 25%.

When the seductiveness of the "certainty" (i.e., the "convincer") feeling guides your response, your brain is not being "user friendly," as Richard Bandler reminds us. As a result we have to learn how to tell good from bad information and the illogical ways we use our mental logic. Too bad for us that we don't have an *instinct* for good quality information. Then we wouldn't jump to the conclusions that we often do.

So! Now you mean that I mind read and I jump to conclusions! Really, sir, I never. . . . !

Rachel, I suppose that you feel certain that you are right. Right?

Indeed I am. You have tried to embarrass me.

But have I succeeded, Rachel?

I AM angry. But not embarrassed.

If embarrassment was the objective, I have failed?

I hadn't thought of it that way.

Now that you have "saved face," let me give you another example. A small gemstone will be handled very differently depending on whether we think it is glass or a diamond. In other words, we act on information based upon our interpretation of what the information means.

Therefore, the quality of the information we act upon is quite crucial and especially so if it involves our feelings. In a case such as the gemstone, most of us would need the expert opinion of someone who can tell a real gemstone from a worthless piece of glass.

Take the old notion of the moon being made of green cheese. In the dark ages, the argument might have gone along the lines that the moon was obviously made of green cheese because God made all creatures of the moon and stars and so on for the use and nutritional needs of mankind. That is a global mind-read. But although it was more common in the middle ages, it is often found today in the average conversation. The interesting part is that the people who thought that way were actually "convinced" of their righteous interpretation of events.

They all had the courage of convictions. Since they operated on faith, they had no need to test their theory. That is one of the reasons that the dark ages lasted so long. The folks all believed they had reality all figured out and explained so they didn't need to look for any other ways to consider the nature of things. Some of the more typical "certainties" were items like these:

A woman's place is in the home.

Buildings will never rise more than 40 stories.

Men should never cry.

Little devils cause disease.

Man will never fly.

The atomic bomb cannot be built.

Mankind cannot get to the moon.

Phobias cannot be cured in five minutes.

IQ is the best measure of a person's potential. . . .

But, sir. I don't think those examples have anything to do with how you handle the class.

What do you mean, Rachel?

Well, those are all old examples from history. But here in class I can tell when you are going to do something embarrassing to one of us.

Indeed, Rachel. And how can you tell?

Very simple. You have a way of knowing when we don't know our lesson for the day and always call on us then to embarrass us.

How do you know I know you don't know?

Because you always *call on me.*

Well, I think that statement makes my point for today. Class dismissed.

CHAPTER EIGHT

HOW A CONSULTING PRACTICE SURVIVES

A client of mine, who is also a friend, recently mentioned a topic of interest to those of us who make a living through the medium of consulting. He received a letter from an erstwhile psychological consultant who wanted an appointment to sell services to my friend's company.

The aspiring consultant wanted to sell my friend on the value of doing therapy on the staff. "Fine," he wrote back, "tell me what it will do for their performance and we'll make an appointment." I anticipated the response . . . none.

From the tone of the solicitation letter it was clear that the consultant did not have any idea about how to handle the problems of performance. It was not that therapy and performance are very far apart. Both fields use behavioral techniques and both result in behavior change. In fact, in many cases, it is very hard to tell the difference between therapy and consulting when one uses the technology of Neuro Linguistic Programming. I could make a strong case that therapy in the usual sense is irrelevant as an idea since the advent of NLP. But I'll save that for another discussion.

Many consultants can't tell the forest from the trees in the field of behavioral science. It is partly a result of many university programs emphasizing more research and more questions rather than the issue of answering the practical questions of our business clients. It is also partly the result of being too close to our profession to consider what we do as a product rather than a profession. (This doesn't even get to the issue of selling the product, which is also an entire subject worth its own discussion.)

As my friend put it, "I see an awful lot of offerings that dance all around the fringes of relevance but not much that gets to the substance of the issues of performance." Possibly a business will search out solutions to their fringe issues, but the bulk of them want to solve day-to-day problems with rather rapid changes in performance. Would an Olympic athlete be given an undetermined amount of time with an undefined program of change to get his act together? The competitive framework of business is no less forgiving than is an Olympic situation. As a result, sports medicine is defined as producing specific effects for the circumstances at hand.

Business needs are just as specific, and behavioral scientists need to know this. But the behavioral science field has not had the kind of hard technology that NLP represents, so many HRD and MD and OD folks have had a hard time making a substantive contribution to business.

A behavioral scientist consultant who does not know that the product must rise to the competitive occasion is very handicapped. The correspondence and junk mail that a business receives from consultants is considerable. Those efforts have a better chance of paying off for the consultant if the product is defined in a way that is relevant to the perceived needs of the decision maker in that business.

One of the handicaps consultants visit on themselves is the attempt to swoon the potential client with the profundity or newness of their offering. New research or new findings by big-name researchers or new concepts are the oft-found mentions in the solicitations. The problems of business, however, are less oriented to newness than one might think. Innovation is important, but the human factor is old news and so are the problems that the folks on the payroll produce as part of their natural behavior on the job. The contrast can be viewed this way: Most university programs teach diverse theories and approaches and take a broad approach to concept formation.

Business, however works best (in most cases) when the options are strictly defined and limited and the actions of the business are able to be reduced to procedures and routines. Therapists and psychologists often try to "expand" people when business wants to focus people. The issue is efficiency and most therapists don't have that in mind as a core value. They are solving for things like potential and growth and other value-laden notions that are great for a seminar in human development but not in the office where routine is usually the rule of the day—not diversity.

In this framework, the issue is not "new, new, new." The issue is the nature of performance. Take a look at your junk mail. You will find that organizations like the American Management Association and others have a collection of offerings that stress the basics of performance in the human resource area.

Topics like performance appraisal, interpersonal communications, assertive skills, basic discipline and others are the staple issues that happen over and over again in business. They are "evergreen" problems and they need solutions to match.

If you are going to work for a business, maybe you should think about what it would take to help make them more successful with your offering than without it. Maybe you should be telling them about the changes you can make in a session or two of coaching. Or maybe you can show them how you can make a difference in a given individual's performance or a group's performance with your expertise.

But then you will need to put a product label on it and be specific as all get out about what it is that you are offering. You might call it coaching, performance management, team building, strategic planning, "process" consulting, organizational development or management development or anything else that matches their needs and your ability.

If you are already successful to some degree, you might ask yourself about the reasons that you think you are successful. And think about how you would describe that success to someone else. Your ingredients are probably going to have something in common with the management population you want to engage in your service. Just what are the similarities? (It's also useful to look at differences, but that is more an issue for analyzing competitors than clients and will not be discussed here.)

You'll find that they have the very same problems your business has even if the client's is on a larger scale. He can't figure out who is the best person to hire, or who should be assigned a given problem, or how to tell someone that their performance is substandard without causing a flap or appearing to be a bad guy.

And as you reread that junk mail, you'll find that there are courses offered in abundance on how to take care of those "human software" problems. Now, if you are a NLPer, you have a new and unique technology that is a major resource for any business of any size. Take a word of caution. You probably won't be able to explain what NLP is, and you don't need to. *I have seen qualified Master Practitioners pale at the thought of trying to explain NLP.* There is no need to go through that kind of ordeal because your client doesn't want to buy NLP; your client wants his problem fixed. And, to boot, he wants the situation fixed to his specifications, not yours.

An awful lot of folks in the last generation have sold things like theory X or Y and self-actualization as a pseudo-religion with the fervor of an evangelist. You are better off being a means to his ends, not a preacher of values. You are not an end in yourself to him. He has other means and some of them will be cheaper.

With problem people, he can transfer, fire, demote, scold or otherwise lower the boom administratively. He doesn't need the elegance of your solution. He needs quick, cost-effective results. He defines his results pretty much in terms of the junk mail you receive from the competition. Titles like "The Disciplinary Interview," "The Performance Appraisal," "Motivating Subordinates" and similar things will emerge in your review.

Those are the "evergreen" products that never go away. Turnover, promotions, and other causes of lowered productivity produce a constant need for solutions to these types of human resource problems.

Consultants who strike out usually do so for very simple reasons. *They offer their mousetrap instead of the absence of mice.* They try to sell NLP, or whatever topic, as the product rather than the removal of an irritation perceived by the client as problems with items like motivation, attitude, skill, stubbornness and so on. So one message is that you don't need "new" to succeed.

When you think about it, it sounds logical. In fact it has been true of the field even though fads have come and gone in abundance. And NLP will be a fad if too many people try to sell it as an end in itself. Some of the fads that have hit the market in the last decade or so are: personnel information systems, quality circles, stress management, career and manpower planning, psychological testing, behavior modification, transactional analysis, and "T" groups. But always, the program fare comes full circle to the basics again. Most fads last a year or two and then a new one comes along.

Times Change

It seems rather like the saying: "The more things change, the more they stay the same." As I look back over quite a few years of the field of human resources, and compare that with the kind of services being offered today, not many things have

changed. Titles, content emphasis and the type of target population vary a little in minor details. But the substance stays
the same.

However, I've changed. Sometimes a really good book or a
speech by a big-wig will raise interests anew in one of the
"evergreen" topics although it will likely be decorated with
new buzz words. The way that has changed me is that I've
learned to adapt to the interests of the marketplace. So if some
guru comes along and stirs up some interest in, say, the power
of positive selling or some other bedazzling topic, I'm going to
take a serious look at how my products or services need to be
repackaged to match the variation on the theme that the
market has taken.

It is important to know that in many cases, client loyalty is
hard to maintain. Products like seminars can age rapidly.
After the middle management of a medium-sized company has
been through your mainstay seminar, how do you follow that
act? They will get pretty bored with your face if your main
package is your only package, in effect.

Still, you have the option of having a spare product or two
in the same vein. Maybe some related one-on-one counseling
would act as a backup to the seminar. Maybe you can stack
your mainstay into beginner, intermediate or advanced levels.

However, the field does occasionally change. Take NLP as
an example. It is truly a breakthrough discovery. Yet all it
does is solve the same old problems faster, cheaper, more relia-
bly and with much more certainty that the result will be what
the client wants and needs. When such a state-of-the-art item
arrives on the scene, things escalate a notch in the hierarchy
of sophistication and complexity.

Computers meant the same thing. They are a pain to use
and they are expensive and complicated and the impact on
business has been pervasive in spite of the initial difficulties
of the transition. Such a case will likely be the course of events
for NLP. An initially difficult entry is likely until managers

are worried that the competition could gain an edge with it. Then they will pounce on it.

It's not really inside information, but I've been writing on management topics for enough years to see the same basic topics parade through about four full-scale cycles. Of course, I have adapted my services to a generous measure to keep up with the market. In retrospect, I don't do the same things exactly, but the themes are there as are the problems a manager has to solve.

Consultants

Let's look for a moment at consultants themselves. There are some rather large general service consulting firms in the behavioral science/human resources/human software field. An example would be Rorhrer, Hibler and Replogle which uses licensed psychologists a lot and serves a generalist's function for the client companies. They offer everything from assessment centers to sales training and lots in between. Then there is Hay Associates which is best known for its compensation services and a variety of assessment and psychological services.

Another biggie is Development Dimensions which works in the prepackaged training and assessment field.

These are all large firms. They have people from all over traveling all over to service just about anything in the field. There are pros and cons as you might imagine. Although they have lots of resources, they also have packages that are expensive to develop and that means they must market the stuffing out of those programs to get their development costs back plus a bit of profit.

That does not leave room for lots of innovation in varying from the design of a program, but replicability is the key to reducing costs and escalating certainty of results.

That means there is a nice hefty market out there for the custom designer. Many companies see themselves as entirely unique. They sort for differences in their thinking between themselves and others. They are folks who are very responsive to the uniquely special program that will fill their sense of their particular needs. The consultant who wants to do that sort of work is going to have to adjust his pricing strategy to allow for the fact that the design is going to take a lot of careful planning and that takes time and that means you are going to have to charge a lot for that service since in this field "time is money" with a vengeance.

Then there is the specialist consultant. Lots of NLPers would qualify for that title. However, NLP is not the product: Performance is the product. The organization needs its people to perform. That is why they are on the payroll. So the question then becomes: What can I do to help people perform better and in what areas will the problems cycle back every so often? If they recycle, then you do not have to invent the wheel every so often. Select the "evergreen" problems and you will find that they do indeed recur.

Look at your junk mail again. Take a company like Fred Pryor Associates. They have a selection of "evergreen" seminars that are one day in length. A particular seminar might be offered twenty times in twenty cities in the space of six months. Well, one thing to be said for that is you will get to travel a lot with that approach. You will see exotic locales like downtown Dayton, Ohio or possibly the romantic garden spot of Biloxi, Mississippi.

In a sense, you must match your marketing rationale and product definition with your temperament. If you are the type who likes to shut off your head at five in the afternoon and forget your work, you are going to offer something very different than the individual who works closely with clients all the way through dinner and the late show at the cabaret. The type of lifestyle you want should be a major factor in your selection of service and the delivery system.

One way to sort this out is to decide the main medium you want to work in. The main choices in the business world are: a case at a time, a program that treats a particular type of problem or a strategic service such as system planning on the order of reorganizations and major system installations. Most folks wind up working in the program or case medium since systems are usually left for the really big operations.

Between cases and programs, however, programs are the more easily marketed. Part of this has to do with pricing. It is easier to sell a ten-thousand-dollar program once than ten one-thousand dollar cases ten times. Some clever folks, however, package their case-oriented service as a program and thus kill two birds with one stone.

Let's look at a couple of examples from my own files since I work in all three of these media. A case usually pivots around an individual whose performance is limited in some way. It might be interpersonal friction, inability to meet deadlines or something along the lines of attitude or motivation. Reframes, strategies, submodalities and related tools are the most likely kind of work you will do with an individual. And in the context of work, the person must be assisted in adapting to the boss' criteria. The solutions might change the individual's planning ability or presentation skills or persuasion skills.

In the medium of programs, the programs could be seminars, or possibly a writing chore such as rewriting a training manual to change its effects using "predicates." A program like the Blessing/White personal growth program is a pleasant combination of interviews, questionnaires and seminars in a closely orchestrated series of activities that result in decisions about mobility that would not have happened so well without the program. Even though it started out as an employee relations package, the clients perceived it as a personal growth program, and so the leopard changed its spots. I've done packages like this in career planning and there is a good deal of satisfaction in producing such a critter.

On the system level there are items like manpower planning. That has a nice dulcet tone to it. It can mean large computer systems to gather up data on the employee population, it can connect to promotion and performance appraisal policies as well as assessment and hiring programs and even termination programs. I've designed and implemented several large systems like this and they are indeed a challenge.

A really comprehensive and integrated system will tie in to the business plans that handle manufacturing, marketing and other functional needs that decide the need for personnel of given qualifications. This level of intervention is not for the amateur. In fact with such a broad scope, the small consulting practice has little chance to even compete in this area.

A point to keep in mind is that as you ascend the hierarchy of these three media from case to program to system, you also switch from psychological to managerial emphasis. The case approach is virtually all psychological in nature, while programs are often a mix of the two. Systems are clearly compilations of programs that are designed to generate decision making data at the demographic level. Items in that repertoire of issues are: How many of what kind of skill do we need at what location and when? That is a very different question than: Why doesn't Harry get along with his staff? That is case-related issue. If you gather up a lot of cases like that you get a program such as: How can we get our supervisors to bite the bullet and really give effective performance appraisals?

All of these items have to do with how the consulting practice survives. You must know what itch you are trying to scratch with your product. You must be able to separate your means from the client's ends. You must know what the difference is that gives you a competitive advantage over people who are offering to solve the same problems but possibly with obsolete methods as compared to yours.

If you are not sure of yourself, ask yourself what it is that you are not sure about, i.e., what is your product, what is the client need, what does the competition offer, and what is the delivery medium of choice. No doubt some manager out there with a consulting budget has the same problem. If you can solve yours yourself and write it up in a nice brochure, then you just may be able to sell it to him. Go out and give it a try. And you will be the voice of authority since it worked for your very best client—yourself.

CHAPTER NINE

CHARACTER STUDIES: MODELING YOUR CLIENT

Is human nature infinite in its expressions? Of course the answer is yes and no. As a primate animal that competes for territory, for mates, and for hierarchical position, our human nature is as predictable as the rising sun. As an adaptive cognitive creature with complex symbolic and body language capability, the range of expression seems virtually infinite. It's not likely, for instance, that we will ever run out of stories to describe ourselves. We use novels, newspapers, textbooks, gossip and-the summit of it all-the soap opera, to study ourselves. Obviously, we find ourselves interesting.

As a practitioner serving clients of all sorts, what are the useful ways to characterize human nature? How do we usefully do character studies or profile personalities or define a person? Personality tests find "traits." Psychiatrists look for syndromes that match the labels in the Diagnostic Statistical Manual. And novelists will often use an "everyman" character to represent and profile selected themes in behavior to tell their story and to have an influence upon the audience.

But, typically, the "moral" to such a story has an erratic ability to influence and change individual habits. Describing the way we are is the writer's outcome and usually the writer will insert a bit of a plug for how we ought to be. Regardless of the origins, such profiles of human characteristics, for all their possible profoundness, don't give us much in the way of prescriptions for changing habits. And it is bad habits that allow us to get in our own way.

For a practitioner to do more than onerously preach personal values, the emphasis must be different. A practitioner needs to profile "character" aspects on the basis of how people learn and change. Prescriptions for change presume that there are specific, effective means to cause the changes in behavior that are at issue. Popular comparisons of character traits on dimensions of glamor or fashionableness, status, brain power, etc. have little to do with one key fact of human nature.

That is, people are always under environmental pressure to adapt to changing circumstances-not to mention adapting to developmental changes in mind and body as we gain experience and age. Every time I visit the dentist I am reminded of changes in my teeth and my bank balance. To make a dent in day-to-day life events, a practitioner needs to profile the person's changeability or adaptability in terms of the change-causing tools at hand.

Changes come in many varieties: moods, relationships, performance, ambitions, values and more. But goals are an area where changes are rather importantly leveraged in their impact on behavior. After all, what one wants is the driving force behind what one does.

Achieving goals, selecting goals or gearing up to pursue goals all imply the fact that our innate purposefulness keeps us hopping around inside our skulls seeking ways to reorganize our thoughts so we can change in ways that get us what we want. Practitioners, by definition, assist others to change and adapt within themselves and within their contexts (or environments).

The author Chekhov has advised us that the writer of novels should know everything about the characters in a story. This profile ranges from family history, the bank balance, the preference for hard- or soft-boiled eggs, the friends, the grades in school and their brand of socks. For an author this makes a person real and, of course, for fiction to work it must be very, very real or we trash the book. The writer needs a full sense of the person. So does the practitioner. But the elements of the profile are very different. Very different, indeed.

What are the tricks of the trade that make the difference between describing behavior and changing behavior? One little trick falls under the category of attitude. An "as if" frame of mind lets us mentally pretend what the results of our work will be. We can mentally figure out what the person will be and do as if our techniques had already been used. We fantasize or simulate the outcome and work backwards to select change techniques to get the chosen outcome—with the client's permission of course. To do this, though, we need to know the person.

Just how and what we do we need to know to pull off our little magic act of causing change? We need ideas about behavior and we need ideas about how it changes. In our practitioners' world we call these ideas models. One way to think of a model is this: A model is a translation of behavior into words (or mental images and symbols, if you like). Mostly we work with patterns in behavior, e.g., how people decide or create or argue or love or many, many other things. So we put those patterns into clusters of words and ideas that represent behavior of both the enduring or changeable varieties.

Which ideas about behavior are useful to make changes? Well, for sure, we know that the bulk of psychoanalytic ideas are pretty useless. Those ideas describe us backwards and explain our limitations in retrospect. But purposefulness is oriented to now and the future—not the past. Common sense tells us that many things do actually change behavior such as illness, marriage, divorce and the arrival of the first child (and not necessarily in that order). The idea of knowing why we are limited is not so handy as knowing how to step into the future without the limitation. We want to know more about how people change, not how they stay stuck.

The positive value of change offers us more than the negative values of limitations. The issue is knowing how change happens within us. These mechanisms of learning and growth are sometimes spontaneous, but clearly, folklore and much of the professional lore about how change works is off the mark or it would not seem to be such a serious and laborious process for so many of us. Let's put one outrageous myth to rest: There is no truth to the notion of "no pain—no gain." Change is easy and natural when you know how. So let's explore a bit and find out some ways to think about the issues.

Since relationships with self and others are part of the Grand Design of homosapiens, it is useful to have models of how those mechanisms of change work. One of the main models I use to sort out behavior is the idea of leverage (the 80–20 rule). The 80/20 rule (also known as Pareto's Principle) is the much-studied idea that 80% of the results of any outcome is the result of a highly leveraged 20% of the actions taken to cause the outcome. Therefore I ask: which behaviors have the most pervasive impact on outcomes? Of course it depends on which kind of outcome you are managing.

Since relationships in human events are pervasive, a biggie is the whole notion of animal dominance. We are a hierarchical animal and it is our nature to form "pecking orders" and to attempt to move up the hierarchy. Solitary animals like tigers or herd animals like cattle don't form hierarchies so there is an important difference here. When we are satisfied (a positive kinesthetic) in pursuit of dominance, we tend to feel combinations of superiority and satisfaction. We have "one-upped" the competition. It's a never-ending process in relationships, and it ties in with goal (achievement) behaviors as well as with how we manage the relationships by turning on and off courtesy and cooperation (both are hierarchically oriented behaviors) as suits us to get a chosen outcome. Of course we are discussing selected motives. Others such as sex, hunger and security are not treated here.

Harvard's David McClelland studied three aspects of our

nature, so I call my use of it the McClelland model. I take 100 imaginary points and "spend" them on three items to profile the preferences of my clients. In particular, I want to know how they act on each of these items as an end in itself from their perspective. It is a handy tool. It tells me plenty-believe me.

Use 100 points and spread them according to your self-assessment of your motives. The first word in each of the three motives is the original meaning of the category with some synonyms thrown in for good measure as additional points of reference to structure the idea.

_____   Power/dominance/competition/politics
_____   Affiliation/relationships/courtesy/cooperation
_____   Achievement/results/goals/objectives
_____   Total = 100 points

This set of motivational preferences is easily sized up in the time it takes to shake hands in many cases once you are familiarized with what details to notice in behavior. The list of items in each category is too long to go into here. Sometimes it takes longer than a handshake. Although if you can't figure it out in another person in five minutes it just means you don't have the idea yet.

This kind of modeling is very useful for a quick way into knowing these facets of the mind and heart of the other person. It is the kind of thing that is often meant when we "get to know a person." Lots of little habits and quirks of personality are gathered up in models like these which have validity and leverage in their components for understanding the other person.

The McClelland model connects to the way people handle dominance. As another aspect of this general type of human behavior, I have constructed another model which I modestly call the Yeagar Power Grid. It accounts for the context we all use implicitly. We always have to adapt to the power moves of others (one-upmanship, put-downs, bossiness, etc.) so that how one does handle power (or doesn't) is important. No one can get through a day without facing this issue unless the person qualifies as a hermit.

The power grid I use as adjunct to the McClelland Model is visualized on a scale of 1 to 10. 1 = Passive (Charlie Brown), 5 = Assertive (Snoopy) and 10 = Aggressive (Lucy Van Pelt and also Attila the Hun, who is quoted as saying: "It is not enough that I win . . . others must lose." That is one of the better lines from the movie *Superman III,* as spoken by Robert Vaughn.)

As you can tell, how one is motivated on these three issues seems very important to me. Of course there are many other motives such as security, hunger, sex, activity and so on. Practitioners develop their own notions of what and how to profile motives. I find these models useful, and that is the test of information developed for character studies: Does your model give you access to change mechanisms within the client that actually make definitive behavior changes? If you can answer "yes" to that question you are ahead of the competition.

Who is the Competition?

The competition for "change agentry," as our work is sometimes called, involves those listed above, i.e., chemistry, surgery, religious conversion and others. And psychologists have claimed some turf on the competitive market and they are coming on strong to offer real challenges to the "establishment" in the form of physicians. Although psychologists are gaining they could do lots better if their tools were as effective as ours, i.e., that is not to say we aren't psychologists . . . lots of us are, including me.

One of the rather antique competitors in psychology is that of "psychological testing." There is a long history of testing in our culture and it naturally has its pros and cons. The statistics can be sophisticated but the rationales are rather tattered and ill-serving to a public hungry for results. I recently read in an issue of *Contemporary Psychology,* the monthly review of new publications in psychology, where the reviewer of another psychologist's book expressed dismay that his author-colleague didn't go to the bother of conducting formal paper and pencil testing sessions on clients for the sake of whatever might be gained.

My distress comes partly from the fact that the test didn't have any productive bearing on the work at issue. Also some well-meaning theorist wanted to put a client through the onerous chore of testing in case something *might* come of it. This "test because we have the tests in stock" attitude prevails after generations of trial and error with testing that has proven to be of very limited value to the consumer.

It is the perfect example of the adage "Give a small boy a hammer and he finds that everything needs pounding." Compared to our skills at pacing and leading and getting *results* in an interview (instead of mere data), I think the reviewer was expressing a pretty common response. It fosters the notion that if one doesn't know what to do to make a change in the client, at least get some data to worry over in a professional paper. In this way, some fame is possible by juggling statistics, even if there aren't any client-changing results. To me that line of thinking is fairly characterized as mental masturbation. It doesn't help the client much but at least the therapist can get off on it. Intelligence testing is another area where things are a lot less developed than in the land of NLP.

For instance, one of the rather unhappy results of IQ testing is that children (and adults, too) are "nominalized." That is, they are tested and "labeled" as being the bearer of a certain IQ. Then the trouble starts. People do have conditioned responses to the meaning of an IQ. Administrators and teachers make routine decisions on the basis of something that seldom correlates with life achievement any better than a politician's campaign promises match the actual delivery on those promises once in office. There is little effective understanding of how the mind's mechanisms of change actually work in this area of "testing" research.

In contrast, when we NLPers use "visual accessing cues," we can routinely teach someone the procedure to be a perfect speller in less than an hour. Using similar techniques, we can change other facets of academic performance that would show up on an IQ test as an increase in "intelligence." Would you consider this an increase in intelligence or would you think that the test wasn't measuring anything of value that related to actual school performance?

An increase in "intelligence" isn't supposed to be possible, according to the theory. Apparently it is thought of as something "pre-wired" like an instinct . . . except when the theorists want to have it the other way. Theorists tend to blame genetics when they don't understand learning or when they can't figure out what is going on.

Instead of "intelligence" suppose we substituted a synonym such as "adaptability." Nature forces all of its creatures to adapt to the environment or to perish. Intelligence might be better redefined as the mental operations that have survival value towards adaptation to environmental pressure.

For my money, the thinking behind testing needs to be overhauled. IQ tests and lots of other tests are based on the same logic as "Galton's mistake." That is, the rationale is based on generating lots of data about a person but the results are statistically averaged rather than individually examined about how a given individual's mental processes actually got that result.

Galton, in 1883, surveyed 100 famous men of his time and asked them about the characteristics of their mental imagery when remembering their breakfast on the day they received the questionnaire. Galton averaged the responses instead of asking how they could be so different within each individual. As a result he missed his chance to have discovered NLP. A common mistake with IQ tests, too.

If someone told you your IQ and asked you to bet on it for its relevancy to your suitability for, say, a job, would you bet your mortgage on it? Or would you bet a month's rent on it? Or would you rather tell people you bet on it but actually keep the money safe in your piggy bank?

The simple fact is this: An IQ test doesn't give a clue about how a mind works. Nonetheless professionals keep fine-tuning a device that is basically useless. It gives no prescriptions about how to raise an IQ. This is partly because the test users assume that an IQ is innate and unchangeable. Any changes are assumed to be the result of statistical error. That means they don't look for sources of change in the scores because it says it is not possible according to their theory.

Nor does IQ directly connect to teaching methods that might attempt to change performance. In other words, it is pretty much irrelevant except for making life hard on the "testee." And, to add insult to injury, no one really knows what an IQ happens to be. It would actually be a lot more useful to insert a dead rat in the individual's record folder. At least we'd know that was useless and no one would be misled into thinking otherwise.

To add fuel to the fire a fellow named Hans Eyesenk, a British psychologist, comes along and blows IQ out of the water on very different grounds. He finds that simple perceptual speed at identifying *contrasts* or *differences* in things corelates .80 or better with IQ scores. If true, that means that speed of perception is the priority variable. Yet others for generations have believed that IQ is the expression of some sort of generic and "general reasoning" power that is also supposed to be innate. It is called "Spearman's G" in honor of the fellow who thought it up.

From the perspective of NLP, we use "strategy" change methods to change things in the client's ability to process information efficiently. We know from our work that strategies are learned and are changeable. We do it every day in our work.

Suppose an IQ test tests for vocabulary and the student's vocabulary is poor because he's never been taught to spell. The result would be that he can't recognize the words on the test. He'd likely score below average on the test. He'd be labeled as "slow" or "low IQ." But, in a ten-minute procedure, I can teach him to spell; he learns the words and his IQ goes up. This isn't supposed to be possible. But I do it routinely in my practice. Of course, the student is relabeled average, but it occurs to me that the tester ought to be relabeled stupid. Neurotic stupidity is the inability to learn from experience. Obviously, the theory is more important than effective thinking.

A friend of mine serves as a wonderful analogy to this process in another field-optics. A close friend of mine for over thirty years, Dr. Ron Reese, was born legally blind due to a rare *in utero* infection. Eventually about 5% of his retina was found to provide him with a tiny fraction of normal vision. For all of the thirty-plus years I have known him, physicians had him look at the classic Snellen eye chart where they put a big letter "E" and other fine print on the wall at a distance of twenty feet away. Consider for a moment that Ron couldn't even see the wall!!! Over the years the doctors "tut-tutted" about how sad it was and gave him prescriptions that improved his reading vision an iota or two.

The parallel to IQ testing is that the doctors held the presupposition that routinely got them to measure such a problem against the criterion of reading acuity. When, in the course of an eye exam, Ron would tell the doctor that he could see better at certain stages in the procedure, his observation was summarily dismissed by the "expert." Ron wouldn't take "no" for an answer. Instead he modeled the way the blind and the field of optics worked and figured out a way to help blind people see. His new method has set the field on its ear and he has improved the vision of previously "legally blind" people by a factor of 500% and more.

The result is that many of the blind are now able to be independent of guide dogs and of being housebound. The doctors weren't able to transcend their theories and notice that the severely visually handicapped needed to see distances so they could get around. The doctors insisted on solving for close-up vision and they also insisted that they knew what was best . . . according to their theory. Their presuppositions were unchallenged. Ron found the flaw in those presuppositions and made a major breakthrough in the field.

In a nutshell, models of your client's and your own thinking can be stultifying or they can be the source for transformation. The difference is in the requisite variety and flexibility in the practitioner's skills. When profiling clients in your mind, the use of models is important. I've described a few such as the McClelland model, the 80/20 rule, the Yeager Power Grid and the horrible example of many IQ tests. In general, the more models you have, the better for your clients.

Even better is when you have a model of your models so you can keep yourself renewing them as your observation skills increase. This way of thinking about modeling and profiling your client's character will help make their infinite uniqueness and expressions nonetheless predictable. Each person has behavior patterns which lead to success, happiness, change and learning. When you discover those patterns, based on your models, and use them, you are on your way to changing failure to success, sadness to happiness and stuckness to performance.

CHAPTER TEN

GOALS: ALMOST EVERYTHING YOU WANTED TO KNOW

A crucial item I work with is a client's goal. The likely fact is that client goals are my *most* important item of concern. The goals are what the client wants and I am there as a professional to help them achieve those goals.

Goals sound simple. A goal is what I want. Right? Not necessarily. A goal may be what you settle for when what you *really* want seems unattainable. A goal may also be so vague and abstract that it is impossible to achieve or define. For instance, "I want to be better!" raises lots of questions. Better at what, better compared to what, better at what time or place and so on.

Answering those and many related questions helps one define a "well formed outcome" (WFO). When I think of those three words, I hear a god-like voice in my mind speaking in an echo chamber to let me know this is *ultimate* stuff. When I ask a trainee "What is the client's well formed outcome?" I like to imagine the trainee is having a similar heavenly experience that communicates the ecstatic importance of the WFO.

A well-formed outcome is, by definition, a result that can be *measured*, touched, tasted, smelled, seen, or heard. Any other kind of goal that doesn't exist in sensory-specific terms (there goes that echoing voice again) is philosophy, not behavior; and we know that philosophy never gives us anything useful to do. In fact philosophy and fantasy are often synonymous in my mind.

The criteria for any goals are that they be stated in positives (*not* "I want to stop worrying" but instead, "I want to feel good,"), that it be within the person's control ("I want to be a Buick" is not in your power), stated in sensory-specific terms (must be able to see, hear, feel, smell, or taste the goal) and that it be ecological for you (King Midas didn't have an ecological wish. Even his lovers turned into solid gold. Some lover *that* would be—a real heart of gold.) And it must be testable (I can prove it works with an objective, verifiable test).

Let's consider your goals in your work whether you are a consultant, practitioner, executive, teacher, or whatever. What do you want to accomplish as an NLP practitioner (i.e. as a "Nelper")?* What do you want to do with your generic skills in human nature? What sort of reception do you want your work to have? Where do you want to work and how much money do you want to make? These are all questions I frequently ask my clients, and they are excellent questions to ask yourself.

Given that there are as many goals as there are people to think them, let's consider two alternative ways to think about goals. In the first case, you might be an unfettered thinker who really believes that the sky is the limit. Possibly you want to be a guru in some breathlessly exciting intellectual trend this year or next: or you want magnificent words to stream from your typewriter as water from a garden hose.

When you write a book about your experiences or a collection of your case histories, you want the book to rise to the top of the *New York Times* best seller list for at least a year, and then to go through a dozen or two paperback printings after having been awarded to the highest bidder in an auction for the movie rights to be played by the biggest name star who is able to portray your sterling character on the aptly compati-

*Nelper—The term used to identify the student of NLP.

ble silver screen. As for the awards that stream in one after the other, you will somehow learn to take it all in stride.

Feel good? You bet it feels good to think about things this way.

On the other hand, maybe you're a lot more laid back about the whole thing. You don't worry much about the outcome of events. You just want to work a day at a time, case by case, week to week as the years roll by. If those experiences and cases eventually add up to a book, that's okay. If lots of folks buy the book, that's also okay. Anything else that happens is alright too. You don't want to impose on the universe; your attitude is pure California, you take things one day at a time, one case at a time, and one page at a time.

There is obviously a difference between these two approaches to setting goals. "Is one better than the other?" you ask. I asked that too, and here's my chance to ask you, class. What's your answer? Okay, class, let's not see the same old hands as always. Yes, Benjamin?

* *The first one wants to do something, Dad, and he's going for it. (It's nice to acknowledge your children in print and Ben is my number one son)*
* Uh huh. Do you agree with that, Rachel?
* *No, Dad, that's unreal. (You have just met my other child who also studies my methods on occasion.)*
* Why do you say that, Rachel?
* *Sounds like a movie magazine to me, Dad. The second person is realistic and has real day-to-day goals. The second is no daydreamer. Eventually, the goals of the second person will all fall into place. It's smart to take things a piece at a time. Friends will tell friends and word of mouth will make the person famous. The friends will ask for a book and . . . .. . you know.*
* And maybe wind up on a TV talk show and be famous and all the other things prescribed for the good life and the American dream, right?

    *   *Well, why not, Dad, that's MY plan!*

Why not? How about the rest of you, class? Give me a show of hands: Which one do you agree with, Mom? (No introduction is necessary here): Linda, are you raising your hand or adjusting your contact lenses? Okay, class, now raise your hand if you agree with Rachel. Ben, why are you raising your hand?

    *   *Just hedging my bets, Dad.*

Uh huh. (He's studying to be a stockbroker.) Well, the rest of the votes are about even. But, sorry Ben, you can't hedge on this one. Neither of these ways is an effective approach for setting goals. Both ways would leave you in the lurch.

Despite Rachel's choice of being existentially in the moment, the second scenario provides only the most limited short-term goals. It's almost as if the future doesn't exist. How can productive efforts add up to a product if there is nothing resembling a plan or way to define the result with an organizing idea? If you don't know where you are going, how will you know when you arrive?

With no overall goal, the outcome, if any at all, would likely be a mishmash of incoherent pieces. Benjamin's choice, in contrast, is at the opposite end of the spectrum. He wants EVERYTHING including the moon and stars, but there is no workable way to get everything because they are not real goals that can translate into actions. The goals are fantasy— not real goals. Ben's goals are too abstract, and Rachel's almost don't exist since they are so undefined.

By NLP standards, a well-formed outcome must be sensory-specific, ecological, within the person's control and testable. The means to acquire the moon and the stars are reserved for the Creator and are not in Ben's control. Hell, there are hardly any jobs for astronauts these days, much less Assistant Creators. Now you may ask about the difference between a fantasy and a goal. Okay, Elana, go ahead. I said you may ask. . . .

* *What is the difference between a fantasy and a goal,
   Doctor?*

Ahh, I'm pleased that you thought to ask, Elana. A goal is
something that can be perceived by the five senses and is not
merely an assemblage of mental images that float idly in your
brain. Thoughts that have no connection to sensory reality are
fantasy. A goal is something you can *achieve*. A fantasy is
something you *want*. Period.

A goal is rather like the mental reciprocal of a question. Can
you NOT think of a pink elephant? Okay, Ben, why can't you
NOT think of a pink elephant?

* *Well, Dad, it's a perceptual trick, right?*

No, not exactly a trick, son, but you're close. It is the nature
of the mind to fill in the "vacuum" caused by a question. Ask
anyone any question that occurs to you and they will answer
in their mind even if they don't want to. Ask anything: What
color are your father's eyes? What did you have for dinner?
The mind cannot NOT answer.

The flip side of this "compulsion to think" is a goal. There
is some choice in goal setting, but once set, the goal serves as
a perceptual alert system and you start to notice all manner
of things that seem related to your thinking in that area of
interest. Scanning a magazine's table of contents makes items
pop out of the page to seize your attention. Before the goal was
set, you'd have skimmed right by such an item.

A goal is a mental magnet that directs attention and thinking toward an outcome. A well-formed outcome (the heavenly
voice did it again) will bring itself into being, by virtue of
innate mental mechanisms, as predictable as the mind's response to a question.

Goals come from dreams—or better yet, goals *are* dreams.
Dreamers in history have been alternatively vilified and glo-
rified depending on the outcome of their dreams. The more
mundane goals that most of us have contain less risk of boom
or bust extremes. But, we ordinary people still use the same

process of transforming a dream into a well-formed outcome and finally into results. The odds are small that we will have an equal chance such as Christopher Columbus to be jeered and then cheered for dreaming *round* instead of *flat*. That's heady celebrity stuff.

Let's trace the elements of a dream. Suppose you want to win the million dollar Pennsylvania lottery. (This choice of topic shows a bit of local patriotism since I live in Bucks County where one of my well-formed outcomes is to have people point at buildings one hundred years from now and say "Yeager slept here." This is so I can one-up George Washington who is said to have slept everywhere in these parts, including in the townhouse next door which is only four years old.)

Of course you want to win the lottery. It is a laudable if somewhat remote goal, but you can indeed imagine any goal you want. You have my blessing. Yet, if you spend your time mentally rehearsing press conferences and driving the imaginary Rolls Royce instead of buying the lottery tickets, your goal qualifies as a fantasy.

In contrast, suppose you do dream of winning the lottery, *and* you splurge a big chunk of your income in lottery tickets. And suppose you work on your subliminal strategies and install the magnetic image that you are ready and willing to win. By the mystic powers of mental magnetism, you start thinking positively to attract the proper cosmic vibrations. You are comfortable that you can handle instant success and won't, at the moment of success, think of trading your pet goldfish for a Corvette.

With the second approach, you might outlive several pet goldfish waiting for the big day, but you'd have a real, honest-to-gosh well-formed outcome. Maybe you would never win, but at least you would be in the running with a goal instead of a fantasy.

By my standard, a well-formed outcome is one of the measures of the good life. The reason is simple: When people want something they have a way of obtaining it. The fact that the goal may not materialize is a fact of life. The insurance industry exists to handle the debris of client goals that have gone afoul. Your own criteria will determine the desirability of a goal and it will find its own place in your own scale of priorities. Criteria are personal. Yet the standards of a well-formed outcome have to be met regardless of your attitude toward that fact. Otherwise, the mind lurches from fantasy to fantasy seeking anchorage in a confusing experience.

Three questions I have learned over the years add credence to a goal.

1) Is the goal *real?* The criteria of a well-formed outcome are the test of this issue. They are, again, positive sensory-specific, within the person's control, ecological, testable, and stated in positive terms.

2) Can I *win* with this goal? Any goal is part of an ongoing process of being supplemented by other goals or is a lesser goal that supports a larger goal. The concern here is: "What is the outcome of achieving your well-formed outcome?" Does it add to your well-being and efforts in ways that you score a win? You may save up money to buy your new car. But if you have to use food money to do it and starve in the process, most folks would not call the outcome a winner.

3) Is it *worth* it? In contrast to other things that might elicit your efforts, is this payoff cost-effective? You might measure this in the forms of feelings, relationships, passions, financial gain, time, energy, resources, or other factors that you might use in pursuit of alternative choices. Do you want to trade off one set of priorities if the payoff is less satisfying than other priorities.

These are common-sense questions that are well worth asking. I became acquainted with these three questions at a seminar that was authored by an engineer-turned-entrepreneur in the training business named Don Schrello. After having assembled literally hundreds of pounds of information documents to support a major product decision, Don realized there had to be a better way to organize information for use in business decisions. The information was too unwieldy to manage.

His astute thinking generated these three questions as a framework to organize the information. He then built a two-and-one-half-day seminar on how to use the questions. In his approach, the three questions are expanded to six sub-questions and they in turn expand into twenty questions. It is rather like the Meta model's cousin for non-human applications. The remainder of the process boils the information down, testing it against criteria, and the information is "scored" against the decision's criteria of the well-formed outcome.

The Process of Elimination in Goal Setting

There is a very strong caveat that needs to be added here. Goals have a funny way of having their dark side as well. When someone has some sort of malfunctioning motivation there can be persistent trouble in trying to get the goal identified. It usually surfaces when someone is conflicted about what they want or about what they think they can get. Often a person will have a goal that they consciously want, but will have a strong program in their mind that stops them from getting it. If someone wants to be rich, for example, but was taught at an early age that money is dirty or otherwise negative, there is almost no chance they will have any luck in achieving the goal.

Another aspect of malfunctioning goals is when someone settles for a lesser goal than they want. There is an interesting aspect of goal setting that happens when an individual settles for a lesser goal for lack of skills to get the goal they actually want. There is a bit of an either/or aspect to the thinking. If the goal doesn't occur on cue in the desired form, the person lowers their expectations unnecessarily instead of learning how to make it happen the way they want or getting needed help.

Usually, in such a situation, environmental changes are used by an individual in futile attempts to stop the bad feeling associated with a goal when there is conflicting motivation. There is a discrepancy between what they want and what their values "allow" them to have. Examples of what people change in their attempts are as follows: lovers, careers, loyalty to a professional school of thought, jobs, automobiles, residence, business partners, religion, lifestyle, and more. Often such changes are subjectively and vaguely perceived as a process of elimination. That is, the limitation is a known phenomenon. And as lists of personal objectives are formulated, those choices which would elicit the feelings of conflict are eliminated from the options of this negative selection process.

Typically, the choice for the person is either to select "successful" objectives with intensely negative kinesthetic responses or to select "unsuccessful" personal goals which are not satisfying, but at least are emotionally tolerable. As one individual stated the issue: "I'd rather be chronically frustrated and a failure than chronically scared out of my wits." That mental set establishes the repetition of the pattern since the "leftover" goals they could handle were not based in choice but in compulsion. They avoid pain: They don't pursue a well-formed outcome.

Similarly, in an episode of the TV serial *Buffalo Bill,* Bill the fictional talk show host makes passes at each female on the scene of the show, and in turn is rejected. He then proceeds, in desperation to avoid a lonely evening, to proposition less and less desirable individuals. Finally, even the janitor is perceived as less painful than a lonesome evening even though the janitor meets none of his criteria of desirable companionship. The janitor is all that is left once other options are eliminated.

The deceptive feature I have discovered in eliciting a desired state (a WFO) is this: a person's image of a desired state is contaminated by their inability to even imagine the well-formed outcome. It is like asking a six-year-old to imagine great sex. It is not in their experience. You will likely have to synthetically construct a well-formed outcome.

Goal Achievement

An illustration that is near and dear to my heart is how I got into the consulting business. For years, I thought I'd like to get out of the corporate rat race and go into business for myself. I had lots of thoughts about it, and even kept my eyes open to the kind of information that would add up to some sort of decision.

The fact that I'd never done anything resembling consulting seemed a little bit intimidating to me. That feeling slowed me down and was the source of endless rationalizations as I stoked the dream but did nothing in particular to change it from fantasy to goal.

I attended lots of seminars and met lots of consultants and time after time I came away with the feeling that I could have done it better. Then one day I made it a point to chat in some depth with the next "headhunter" who was to try to lure me from my current employer to another. (The headhunter gets a healthy fee for finding management talent.) I told him of my pipe dream and he was (as I anticipated in reading his body language) willing to discuss the topic of how he had gotten into the field and gave me lots cf invaluable advice about the pros and cons of the consulting life style.

Since I had negotiated a four-day work week at my then-current job (that is a story of its own worthy of *Ripley's Believe It or Not*), I arranged to hang out with the consultant and did some chores for him to be able to learn a bit about his work.

Lo and behold! He mentioned me to one or two of his clients and one thing led to another and soon I was into the consulting world feet first and busier than I'd ever hoped to be in my fantasies. You might well ask: "What does that prove?" It proves part of the oft-heard logic that goals work in ways that we can predict. There are at least two very important aspects to goals. The conscious and unconscious aspects of goals are what I'm referring to. (Oops, I've split an infinitive.) On a conscious level, you usually make a list of the things you want, then you figure out the steps you need to take to bring the goal into being.

If you tell yourself that you want to do a particular thing, like be a consultant, or anything else, you begin to accumulate information about the topic in day-to-day experiences. You might have casual conversations or go to meetings and seminars with a focused mental set that acts a lot like a magnet to direct your attention to notice things you'd have ignored in the past.

At the same time, you are programming your unconscious mind by virtue of this focused attention. You are telling your unconscious mind that you want this particular result and things start to happen. When your eyes scan a magazine's Table of Contents you tend to notice things you'd have ignored before. (Few ever miss the centerfold, it seems.) These little attention grabbers give valuable direction to things because you have actually programmed your unconscious to direct your attention so that it just seems natural to notice these things.

You won't sense any effort, you'll just do it automatically because the goal has your mind engaged to get you what you want. This focus also keeps your mind from scattering its resources and brings things together for you. When you are hot, your mind will let you know by leading you to situations and information that is in the vein you need to achieve your results.

An easy way to study this effect is to sort out the Liberal Arts graduates from the Business Administration graduates at any given college and notice their attitudes about money.

The business grads clearly are going into business because a majority of them want to make money. . . . usually lots of it. And they do. Then study the liberal arts graduate who is into other values of service, aesthetics, and so on. They do not especially want to make money, although, a few do in spite of themselves. Most do OK, but they don't have the accumulated wealth of the business types over a five- or ten-year period.

Check it out. It boils down to the fact that, motivation being in good condition with no conflicts, both types get what they want. I find this to be true. In a nutshell, there IS power in thoughts. When you put out a thought into the universe, (assuming your mental machinery is unconflicted and in good working order), you will get what you want. A lot of those flower children of the sixties are tired of being aesthetic and intellectual if they can't afford a decent Japanese car, and are now reprogramming themselves to want money . . . and it works for them, too. They call it prosperity or abundance consciousness.

Of course they still work like the rest of us do, i.e., a day at a time, but they have sent their mind a message to think longer term and in specific ways to develop the new agenda to what is wanted. The unity of thought begins to happen with the well-formed outcome. The specification of any goal brings it closer, and when it is united with thoughts at the conscious and unconscious level, the odds of achieving the goal are increased at least ten-fold. . . . and that is a better deal than buying a lottery ticket.

CHAPTER ELEVEN

WHAT??!! ME WORRY?

Good morning, class.
Good morning, sir.

At the start of a new NLP training program, it is useful to talk about the worries you have about the program. Let's start this way: May I please have a show of hands if you have had any fear or worry about doing well in this program? Thank you very much, class. You can put down your hands now. Benjamin, I notice you were the only one in class who didn't raise your hand. (Please note, he is my son and an NLP practitioner.)

I was worried that you'd call on me, sir.

I suppose that's understandable, Benjamin. Most of us are afraid to admit that we are scared. I'm pleased that you were able to admit it with a bit of prompting. Being scared and not dealing with it can leave us in the lurch. Did you notice the way the worried feeling stopped you from noticing much of anything else, Benjamin?

Well, I suppose you're right, sir.

Yes, indeed, I enjoy being right as you can imagine. But the important thing is to notice that being afraid and then being afraid to do anything about it is quite an uncomfortable place to be. Right, Benjamin?

(Mumble, mumble).

What's that, Benjamin?

I said: I was afraid of this, sir.

I see. You mean I'm embarrassing you now?

Uh huh. You might say that.

OK, then, I'll say that. "I'm embarrassing you."

(Arrrgggghhhh. . . . mumble mumble).

In spite of your concerns, Benjamin, this is not a test. It merely points out that as long as you have a strong negative feeling about something, it is very hard to get much accomplished while you are in that frame of mind. Wouldn't you agree, Benjamin?

(Mumble, mumble).

How's that again, Benjamin?

I was wondering how I could become invisible.

Not to worry. We'll go on now that the point is made. One of our purposes here is to bring your worries out into the open, class. After all, they are only feelings and as you just observed, Benjamin did not melt nor did anything else devastating happen to his person. Although, common wisdom propounds the notion that bringing fears and worries out into the open will do much to defuse them, this is obviously not always the case.

Ask your average bartender. He or she will tell you that they hear the same worries over and over again from their customers.

It is true that some fears are dissipated that way, but seldom are the big glitches of life erased so easily from one's repertoire of distressing events. Yet it is a comfort to know that you are not the only worried individual in the class. Were the rest of you relieved when you saw the other hands go up along with yours?

Except for Benjamin's sir.

Except for Benjamin's, Rachel. Indeed. (My daughter, as you might expect.)

Only occasionally do people like to stand out, especially if they are afraid of being the only nervous person in the room. Experience tells me that most people new to NLPing are a bit nervous at first. And that means it is not the trademark of the neophyte since we have so many master and doctorate degrees in the class. After a short while, a beginning NLPer gets some measure of comfort in handling the complexity of the field and they give many reasons. Although I have little use for reasons, since they are often excuses clients use to stay stuck, there are some interesting criteria to announce to the inner self about how well things are going. Among mine are: when I'm NLPing I get a sense of satisfaction, it's a living, it's a modest source of pride, it makes me smile a lot and, often, it scares the hell out of me.

I don't think there is such a thing as a fearless NLPer or anything else for that matter. Even in the most classic Western movie, John Wayne was the first to admit being scared before the shoot-out. The part the movies leave out is that "scared" is not a signal to go macho. It is a signal to pay attention to what you are doing. As Linda Sommer says, "It is a signal to notice what you are not noticing." Being scared is the unconscious mind's way of telling you to do something useful instead of something habitual.

Anxiety is emotional radar warning you of dangerous shoals on the horizon. Since the brain, as Richard Bandler has pointed out, is not user-friendly, being scared usually means you are about to engage in an activity that you are not mentally organized to handle effectively with your usual aplomb.

The message is: use the feeling as nature intended . . . as a signal to reexamine your attitude, situation, skills, goals or anything else you can think of that may be relevant. To me, courage is figuring out what you need and then making sure you go for it. It is one of the things you will learn here. I know it will be hard to believe, class, but even I have worries. Yes, indeed, I do.

I worry that I may fall behind in a very fast-track field. Sommer, Dilts and Bandler, for instance, are fierce intellectual competition. I worry that I may not have anything useful to say. I worry that I'll repeat myself, *ad nauseum.* I worry that no one will give a damn about what I have to say or that

I'll say it with excruciating dullness. I worry that the class clown will complain to the management about me in a nasty letter and depress me for several moments. (Since I am the management here it is a double bind I might never be able to reconcile.) I worry that what I have to say will not prove useful to the audience.

I could go on at length. But the value of these little worries (and they are little since I am usually healthy and safe from the elements and from fluoridated water) is that they motivate me initially to do something specific about making sure that nothing substantial comes of them. I prepare and I make sure I know my stuff. The worries are a warning that I have to get my act together. That's all they mean. There is no deep psychological significance. Nature made worries to be our early warning system. Worrying is emotional radar. (It is also future pacing with a negative kinesthetic, if you are already among the cognoscenti of NLP.)

It is often believed that what we don't know won't hurt us. I don't subscribe to that view. I like to look at things straight on even though I may be oblique in how I tackle them. Let me give you an example. Years ago I knew I was not going to make a career out of the normal corporate life style even though I was doing exceptionally well at it. In one job I was twenty years younger than any comparable executive in the field. I wanted to go out on my own as a consultant. The thought had a siren call quality to it. And it also scared me out of my Ivy League suit. I was bored with endless meetings and interminable delays for the consensus "votes" that decided everything from the size of an office to the thickness of the toilet paper.

I realized that I had to get out, but I was making a pretty penny there. Enter the "Golden Handcuffs" that are spoken of with such mixed feelings in the executive suite. It occurred to me that I'd have to figure out a pretty good idea to make on my own what those misguided folks at the top were paying me. Simple arithmetic made it pretty clear that to keep up my standard of living I'd have to charge some hapless organizational client about $1,000 per day for a lot more than 50 days a year just to break even.

Then the thought struck me that I might not know anything that was worth that much money. Enter a very big worry. I couldn't stay and I couldn't get out . . . at least not yet.

To shorten the story, after a year or so I had figured out some products that were pleasantly lucrative and met my criteria for repeat business, intellectual challenge, and avoidance of the unemployment line. I did my homework and finally entered the marketplace as a full-fledged consultant and NLPer with a portfolio of credentials to put me on the map as a hungry and dependable resource for my clients.

Did I worry? You bet your birdcage I worried. It drove me to my version of success. Could I have done it without the worry? I don't think so.

But as soon as I knew what the fears were all about (spurs in my thick hide as it turned out), they weren't fears any more but the fears changed to excitement and anticipation. Fortunately, I had a program in my head that allowed me to enjoy the commotion after I figured it out. Some people need that program installed in them. Scared can be changed to fun. It can be done as a challenge and not a threat.

Now if I hadn't . . . yes Rachel?

Aren't you going to tell us how much money you make?

I'm afraid not, Rachel. Now, as I was saying. The notion of listing your fears when you're worried can help a bit. You might want to write down your worries if you are visual, or talk them over with a friend if you are auditory and so on. Now, what are some of the fears that I anticipate this group will have? I know you'll be pleased to learn there are quite a few based on my experience with other would-be NLPers. This means there is lots of room for progress. Neophyte NLPers worry that:

-I won't identify the client's real problems.

-Letting go of my traditional training will leave me tool-less.

-I'll impose myself on the client.

-I won't impose myself on the client (some people like it both
 ways).

-I won't use the right techniques.

-The client fix won't last.

-I won't be observant enough.

-I won't know what to do.

-I won't be able to apply the techniques to myself.

-I'm too hung up in my own issues to be any good.

-I'm too. . .. . .

Let's quit. That's enough. Once you've acknowledged your
worries you can plan to deal with them.

How to start? Cautiously. Of course you have hopes that you
will succeed. But likely as not the worry will be there as you
think through your plans. Hope is simply a mental simulation
of the future with a positive feeling. Worry is a mental simulation of the same future with a negative feeling. A realistic
attitude is usually a simulation of the future with no strong
feelings either way.

Yet, if you are not at least a little afraid of trying, you may
be dissociated enough to play the role of Mr. Spock in the next
Star Trek movie.

So I started off in the field of Career Planning and was
enchanted by the wonderful results and then just as quickly
realized that the product would be as dead as mutton in eigh-
teen months due to the nature of that marketplace. I had to
find a product that was "evergreen." Enter NLP. It was a
product that dealt with human nature itself. "How to get
people performing" was the way I framed it. I was worry-less.
I knew that human nature would not go away. It was here to
stay and so was NLP. Ahhh.

Finally. An enduring product.

But I spoke too soon. Murphy was right with his pronounce-
ment that "Nature always finds the hidden flaw." It was a
complex technology. I had to learn it and I had to sell it and
I had to stay on top of the field and . . .. . . It seems like I'll be
doing NLP into retirement. But I'm not worried about it any-

more. There is *always* an outcome. I have confidence that
things will work out.

Yes, Benjamin?

*Well, Dad, does that mean I can have the Corvette to keep at
college?*

Benjamin, I was worried that you'd ask that.

CHAPTER TWELVE

IDENTIFYING PATTERNS IN CLIENTS

Mom, apple pie, hot dogs, Pogo, JFK,—each name elicits a vivid mental image from personal experience and its unique personal meaning. It is a fair question then to ask: "What's in a name?"

Etomologists, English teachers, grammarians, and linguists will each recognize various nouns as representing different phenomena of unique characteristics. They will then classify them according to some system of pigeon holes that represent some aspect of their world.

If, on the other hand, we were biologists, we would use words and start to classify a list of creatures according to some scheme. Say, tigers, eagles or horses, while a Nelper might use words like fortuples, anchors and so on.

What does it mean when you select intervention techniques to match a particular label? Hopefully, the labels and techniques match the client's subjective reality. The reason is simple. *The label serves as an organizing principle for your thinking.*

As species of animals differ they tend to be given various Greek or Latin names. Animal species may differ by size, shape, color, camouflage, dominance patterns, bone structure, teeth patterns, communication modes and so on. Yet for all the effort that goes into separating creatures (and in NLP, verbal and non-verbal language) so that their meanings are useful to us, there are problems. For our purposes, we will focus on the relative meaning of the word labels we give to things we can observe in behavior.

In the world of NLP, we ask questions like this: How can we tell the difference between a fortuple and a strategy? Or how can we tell the difference between a modal operator and a universal quantifier? Or the difference between a phobia and a compulsion? The question of what constitutes a category of a specific phenomenon can become a little bit complicated. Categories are also relative. They change in meaning and priority depending on your purpose and many other things.

For example, a phobia and a skill are both compulsive behaviors for the most part. They are different in that the skill is under conscious control and the phobia is not. Sometimes compulsions and skills go hand in hand. Sitting up straight in a chair and not falling out of it is a skill. If you don't think it is also a compulsion, notice the compulsion you feel to resist if you were to try to let yourself fall out of that chair. Maybe only Chevy Chase has the slapstick ability to willfully override that compulsion.

A phobia is a behavior that compels you to avoid a negative experience such as confronting a phobic object like a large Doberman Pinscher. A comparable item like chair-sitting is also a compulsion that keeps you from falling over. They are both compulsive and in a general way they are the same. Yet they are different in the feeling associated with them.

Phobias have negative feelings associated with them while skills have a positive feeling associated with them. That issue of feeling is the essential difference. We like the good feeling and hate the bad one. As conventional logic goes, the one we like is called a skill and the one we don't like is called a symptom. To my mind, that is thinking with a forked tongue.

By labeling the negative feeling as a symptom, many professionals will not look on the phobia as a skill, it will be called "pathology." But pathology is still largely mysterious to the therapeutic community. Thus changing the label handicaps the practitioner with a mysterious process. Skill is hardly given a second thought. Since that pathology label implies a whole gaggle of professional meanings, the person with the phobia will be managed differently than a person with a skill deficiency since pathology is the more "serious" of the two.

If you don't think a phobia is a skill, ask yourself what it would be like if you could remember the grocery list with the same skill and repeated precision that you use to exercise your phobia. No one ever forgets to use a phobia on cue. Do you remember your loved one's birthdays with such guaranteed certainty? As you can see, the name we apply to something has a lot to do with how we respond to it. You might even make the case that willpower is the distinguishing feature. Without willpower, it is a habit or compulsion. With willpower it is a skill. And in NLP, willpower is a function of choice and skillful programming of the mind.

An advantage of NLP over other behavioral approaches is its efficiency in producing behavioral change. One source of its comparative efficiency and effectiveness is the premise that observing patterns in behavior is more useful than theorizing about behavior. The data base of a theory tends to get lost in a jungle of circular "wordsmithing."

Many a professional has made a career of studying word phantoms that have no behavioral correlates. They might have been more productive as poets, I think. Yet, this is partly because the flexible nature of language means that the linguistic meaning and definition of any given behavioral phenomenon is relative to the observer.

We often want to find patterns in ourselves as well as our clients. After all, our work is reciprocal and recursive. For example: aggression to one observer is defined as assertive by another observer. Since meaning is relative, you must pin down what you mean. Thus there is a need to establish "operational definitions," a tradition in behavioral science research seldom done precisely in behavioral science practice. The nature and use of operational definitions (i.e., naming a specific observable phenomenon) must be factored into the practitioner's rationale or, if you like, the practitioner's taxonomy.

You may think the names you choose for behavior are small potatoes. If so, I'll ask you, the reader, this question: What do you notice at this moment about your surroundings? Assuming you are in a room, did you notice the chair you were sitting in before I asked? Or did you notice the colors, the textures, the lighting and shading, odors, telephones, sounds or the taste of the air? Most of them would only come to your attention if there were some immediate cause to draw your attention to them.

The point is that you will focus your attention toward finding and noticing the things that are related to what you are "ready" to notice.

As a final item, did you notice the light switch? And are you likely to notice light switches for the rest of the day now that I ask you to do so? Check it out. You will find it hard not to notice light switches since it has been brought up. A label draws your attention to items related to your focused motivation the way a magnet draws iron filings to itself.

What's in a name? Lots. If you are not convinced by now, take my word for it. A word is a map and that map determines how you plan your trip. And a diagnostic label is also a map. And like any map, you must allow for testing its validity as you go along to ensure that it matches the territory as you progress.

Discrepancies usually mean an inaccurate map, not a perverse reality. Also it is worth noting that different mapping techniques will produce different information. A photograph of any given scene will look very different depending on whether it is photographed with color film, black and white, infrared or X-rays. It may well be the same abstract reality, but it will be handled very differently depending upon your methods and purposes.

Often I get curious about the effects of how the practitioner defines and labels the behavior of the client. The definition or model used to interpret behavior significantly determines the value and usefulness of the procedures you select to manage the issues presented. The tentative meaning of the client's behavior depends on how the practitioner initially defines and interprets it. Defining or categorizing client behavior uses a specific set of procedures.

For instance, you use rules of thumb (i.e., models) to interpret the meaning of those sensory-based observations. We base our efforts on the behavior, i.e., fourtuples. Language labels streamline communication about the behavior. Still no two fourtuples are alike, even if they are close enough to merit the same label.

To match the client's behavior with a label that "covers all the bases" of that behavior, you need a wide array of models to choose from. Labels that are in common use are phobia, compulsion, depression and so on. You might also keep in mind that in many cases the diagnosis can be the cure. In medicine, it often happens that as a gynecologist explores a woman's fallopian tubes to study fertility, the instruments will unplug a blocked tube in the process of the examination. In asking clients organized questions, many a client is "reframed" in the process and cured.

Diagnosing client behavior has evolved from the vagaries of an art form to the procedures of a technology with NLP. The specific procedures used to identify the patterns that limit performance and individual effectiveness are the observe of the correspondingly specific procedures used to evolve a client from limitations to fully developed capabilities. How do we tell these items from one another? The same way a taxonomist would. We look for similarities and differences that are systematic in their variations.

The fact is that in this discussion, I am "making up" the whole idea of how to think about these issues. I'm creating "nominalizations" to label phenomena that mean something to me according to my own systematic observations. The fun part is that you can make up labels like this, too. This is also how science works. Scientists make up words to label things they observe or hallucinate to be possibilities in the real world. They call it a theory, and if they are good at their work, they will figure out a way to test their idea.

The only glitch in this set-up is if the scientists do low-quality work and try to explain their theory (usually about why it doesn't work) rather than to try something else.

The compulsion to explain rather than rethink cause and effect is an unfortunate tradition in parts of behavioral science. It largely comes from the mentality of "right vs. wrong" instead of "different than expected." What if Flemming had considered bread mold "wrong" instead of as a curiosity? Thus we have an advantage in NLP because we use modeling which is a more direct sensory-oriented way of trying to figure out how things work. It is also easy to make a case that NLP tends not to use labels at all when working with a client.

Again, the reason is that NLP works with "fourtuples." A fourtuple is the actual behavioral unit being observed. It is important to know that the behavior of each person is unique so that any label is only going to be a rough approximation of what that same label may mean if it is applied to someone else. Often we get stuck in this issue of labeling if we have a conditioned response to the names and labels we are working with.

For instance, if we say the word "deviant" we get a different response than if we say "unconventional" or "different" or eccentric or maverick. Each label has its own associated meanings to any given individual. All imply differences from the norm. Some have negative feelings associated with them. Most likely "eccentric" will produce a benign smile while "deviant" will produce a frown.

But how do we name a symptom or a syndrome? This is quite a subject as it turns out so we will only touch on items directly related to this discussion. In summary, the main notion is that the label represents observable behavioral distinctions that are "sensory-based" verifiable, shared information. Anything else is an opinion and, like noses, everybody has one whether it works or not.

In this discussion, I am modeling some of the things I do. These things have the virtue of replication by someone who shares the coding structure that NLP uses to play with information. Models can be generalized or otherwise applied to the issues that confront a practitioner on a day-to-day basis. Modeling presupposes a bit of curiosity.

One of the things we don't want to do is to model only one way to do things or to take too seriously the models we assume to be true. That is a sure way to proving that the world is flat. The evidence all leaned that way if you had a flat-earth mental model. If you changed to a round-earth model, a lot of the other things suddenly became possible.

Consider, for instance, the ability to get home delivery of a pizza in Philadelphia. Philadelphia's pizza potential remained undiscovered long after the round-world model came to prominence. Possibly folks were slow to see the franchise potential of pizza shops in the New World.

No doubt, many behavioral scientists will be able to prove NLP doesn't work or that it is a mere collection of techniques that are more profound within the framework of their own favorite theory. They are entitled to their theories. Theories are useful, however, to "explain" or to cover up therapeutic failures with notions like "the resistant client" or "unresolved transference". . . . . enough on that, let's go on.

A simple model and word label I find useful to discuss here is that of *conflict.* I have worked a gaggle of cases recently where I used conflict as the touchstone label to test my thinking when, superficially, it did not seem to be an issue. With only a slightly different mental set, I might have jumped to other conclusions and used a model of phobia or trauma or strategy or something else to make sense of a client's issue. I'm glad I didn't. I modeled them carefully and came up with lots of conflict. Here's some of what I've learned about labeling fourtuples.

Seven Clients

Identifying the model that best matches a client's issues means sorting through lots of possibilities like those mentioned above (i.e., phobia, conflict, etc.) and testing your idea. After working with a series of clients with very different issues and stories, I found, in retrospect, a common denominator to their complaints: conflict.

Similar to the rationale of Universal Reframes developed by Linda Sommer (1983), a recurrent pattern was noted among many clients and proved to be a highly leveraged source of positive change. Here are seven abbreviated descriptions of "conflict" cases that characterize how differently things can appear on the surface.

CLIENT #1: A teaching professional with outstanding credentials was employed in a stable position, but could not effectively develop a part-time consulting practice. The conflict emerged this way: "I want to have more money, but I don't want to be crass enough to go after it like a merchant."

CLIENT #2: A small-business owner was achieving only break-even results from extensive efforts and held a series of menial part-time jobs to make ends meet. The conflict: "I want to be independently successful but I need nurturance and to be dependent on authority figures."

CLIENT #3: A manager in a large financial organization held a stable position, but was not advancing and developed intense psychosomatic symptoms. The conflict: "I want to have a manager's status but I don't want to take the responsibility of leadership."

CLIENT #4: A certified helping professional was operating a marginal private practice and holding menial jobs to produce additional income. The conflict: "I want to work with people, but I don't like or trust them."

CLIENT #5: A small business owner was doing poorly with the latest in a series of attempts to run a holistic-oriented service. The conflict: "I want to run my own business but I need someone to boss me and motivate me."

CLIENT #6: An out-of-work specialist was considering opening a health-oriented service that had no consumer appeal, an undefined product and no clear financial objective. The conflict: "I want the higher earnings of my own business, but I don't like to worry about the insecurity of worrying about business ups and downs."

CLIENT #7: A successful businessman had difficulty with occasional sexual impotence. The conflict: "I want to sleep around but I feel guilty about it."

The client issues covered a wide spectrum of other topics besides conflict, although conflict was by coincidence the major issue in the initial session. Without fully representing the many details of these cases, they will nonetheless illustrate a few points as we move along through the ideas.

Looking for Leverage by Chunking Up

Often, in the initial interview, a client will ask for a rather modest change in behavior such as: "I want to be more organized" or "I want to relate to people better" or "I want to earn more money" or a host of other specific content issues. The requests have the generic form of "Help me succeed at _____." Possibly, you will want to do many things such as collapse an anchor or two or reframe an inhibiting part.

Typically, this conscious representation of a presenting problem (and its reciprocal, the well-formed outcome, the goal, or the desired state) can deceive the practitioner into solving the superficial form of the issue as presented by chunking up only one level instead of two or three hierarchical levels of abstraction in information levels to a more comprehensive or generic model.

Chunking up is a mental procedure for generalizing data

and comparing it to conceptual models thought of in a hierarchy of increasingly generalized (or abstract) comparisons. If not constantly tested against the client's fourtuples, abstract labeling can deviously distort into a mere theory. Certainly that would be counterproductive. The base line is always observable fourtuples and the abstract information hierarchy can be scaled up (macro) or down (micro) from there.

The result of solving the presenting problem as stated can result in an unnecessary series of sessions where the content of the problem changes but the form or structure of the problem remains constant at a more general chunk level. A series of six or seven client sessions may present a list of content issues the client wants to be resolved such as the following: Session 1, Creativity; Session 2, Optimism; Session 3, Sensitivity to others; Session 4, More productive; Session 5, More efficient; Session 6, Better memory; Session 7, etc.

If I think in layers, I can use this illustrative and arbitrary model of several chunk levels in decreasing generality from A to D. You may already do something similar.

A.   Models to interpret and synthesize data: Predicates, Accessing Cues, Conflict, Trauma, Phobia, Anchors, etc. (Interpretation level).

B.   Techniques to elicit data: Observation, Questions, etc. (Stimulus level).

C.   Client behavior: Verbal and Non-verbal content, etc. (The event level also known as fortuples).

D.   Therbligs: the smallest observable components of an event (as expressed in the components of a fourtuple such as a submodality).

Experience and testing will tell me if this model of a component of my own modeling is useful. The ideas I put into this sort of model change frequently, but it will do for now to illustrate ideas.

Of course it is taken for granted that the practitioner will "Meta model" (level "B") the meaning of these client "nominalizations." A nominalization is a word label representing an observable phenomenon. An important characteristic to note is that just as a label on an office file folder represents what is in the file, it is not the same as the content of the file. Two people using the same name for a file (i.e., "Invoices") will have different content due to different situations.

Nonetheless, the practitioner may "fall into process." This means that the practitioner pays more attention to what the person says than to how they say it. This risk occurs at the "event" level (level "C") without exploring the meaning at a larger (level "A") conceptual "chunk" level. At level "A" one is exploring for a common denominator. Otherwise, the practitioner can wander through an endless series of minor changes or "fixes" that have relatively little impact or significance to the client.

The outcome of too much small-chunk thinking is a series of sessions that produce incremental change, but not leveraged change or pervasive impact such as an altered lifestyle, changed relationship, or career acceleration. The idea that covers the most psychological "bases" in the client has the possibility of providing the most pervasive changes by virtue of being the most comprehensively matching map.

Models and Rules of Thumb

In contrast to solving in small-chunk bits and pieces, the leveraged goal produces self-generating changes in the client that will operate independently of the practitioner. This is because it transcends the content level of the presenting problem and the chunk level of conscious experience.

To do this you can chunk up to a model that has a larger frame of reference. Without digressing to the subject of modeling at this point, it should be sufficient to point out that in the cases referenced here, different models might have been used successfully.

Although no model is comprehensive for all client concerns,

some generic processes occur more often than others. For example: A phobic model might be applied if the person seemed phobic about success (as many of these might have seemed) since that is a popular "catch-all" notion in the feminist movement. Such cultural fads in thinking can be misleading. One might generalize to think that the client's achievement has some negative meaning or has disastrous, if unnamed, consequences.

The client often will experience the issue only as a bad feeling or an inability to do or to stop doing something. A practitioner might also have defined the problem in these cases as being a dysfunctional motivation strategy. Granted, not enough detail is being presented here to make it possible to even consider these or other alternatives. The point is merely to lead to related issues that will follow in due course.

As it happened, the model in these cases that was found a best match for exploring the larger-chunk frame of reference was the notion of "conflict." Conflict was used as the rule of thumb or the common denominator applicable to the various problems and specific content manifestations offered by the client on entering the interview.

The question I asked is this: Is conflict the primary source of the responses they wish to change? Is it the leveraged way to define the issue and produce the highest ratio of effort to results? It was certainly pervasive in these cases as it turned out. Yet it might have been a different answer if the client issues had been configured differently. Therefore, as in many aspects of NLP, the content of the client answer is less important than asking well-formed questions and testing the answer.

Even though conflict was not the only potentially useful model in these cases, the conflict model was the fulcrum of the 80-20 rule (also known as Pareto's Principle). The 80-20 rule says that 20 percent of your effort produces 80 percent of your results. Part of my message is to observe for interventions that have such a potential for leverage in them.

How did I decide in particular to use conflicts as a source of leveraged change in these cases? Part of my strategy is to look for incongruities and asymmetry in body language and para-language patterns. Incongruities are reasonably certain indicators of what I call conflict. For example, shoulders that are not held level, asymmetrical facial patterns, or sequential verbal tics such as "No, yes . . . I want to be better."

In the above sample list of content issues, the practitioner might repackage the detailed list of desired changes into a large-chunk (and positive) definition of the problem as: "I want to know how to be more successful at achieving my goals." Of course, I will also look for an answer to: Are you "allowed" to have these goals, or are they the only viable goals for you? Or are they the goals you've set in ignorance of other possibilities?

Those content goals might manifest themselves in many ways. As suggested above, the client might want creativity, optimism, sensitivity, and so on.

It is given that many pervasively operating Meta programs (comparable, say, to the Transactional Analysis "Life Script"), established at a younger age, can continue to operate "out of context," out of consciousness and unsatisfyingly for an adult. These are often a source of conflict between what is wanted vs. what one learned at an early age as acceptable behavior in the context of childhood.

Pattern Identification

An issue in such cases as these is an incongruity between the client's poorly formed conscious objectives and powerful unconscious objectives. They say they want "x," but sensory observations do not confirm the statements.

How to do this: In the first scan of behavior, sorting is done to identify the positive, neutral and negative kinesthetic responses to the spontaneous descriptions of the present state and desired states. Of course, I observe for incongruities of body language and story rationale. For example, one client wanted to marry and settle down. The description was sober. When he described his current singles lifestyle, he was animated and smiling.

The discrepancy led me to probe a great deal more and uncovered a conflict in his beliefs about casual sex and enduring relationships.

Eliciting these client descriptions reveals Meta model violations that must be further sorted. I prefer to use the Yeager Performance Model (1982) as a guide to formulating Meta model questions. The model labels issues in terms of whether the person is limited by lack of know-how, lack of opportunity or lack of unfettered motivation. Another idea is to look for the reciprocal of an issue. For example, a common pattern is for a person to blame others for behavior that they recognize and dislike in themselves (projection).

Either/Or Thinking

Consider this double bind presented by many clients: "Either I am inexpressive and shy and the payoff is to be approved, but also goal-frustrated, or I am expressive and heard and the payoff is to be disapproved (K-) and goal successful." A typical case is the person whose success makes them feel guilty, rejected, alone, aggressive, unwholesome, etc. The option of being expressive and approved (K+) has been rendered inaccessible and therefore deleted from the individual's response potential.

The practitioner then would appropriately search for the occurrence of an event to serve as a resource anchor where the client was expressive and in positive kinesthetics and stack and install it as a behavioral option.

By being locked into only one behavior on a spectrum of possible behaviors, the person can, perhaps, imagine effective behaviors as desired states, but cannot engage in them due to the intense negative kinesthetic that prevents them from accessing the remaining options on the spectrum. Generically expressed, the person wants to be "X;" but if "X" is achieved, then they are (by definition of prior conditioning) also "Y."

Experientially, "Y" is somewhere on the continuum under the influence of negative kinesthetic meaning. This phenomenon takes various forms, but unconscious Modal Operator or Cause/Effect violations are typical.

Modal Operator: It is unacceptable to be "Z" (K−)

Cause/Effect: If I am "Y" (K+), that also makes me "Z" (K−)

Y = Successful as defined by the client's desired state

Z = Negative kinesthetic images

Chunking up a level of generality reminds us that words are models and abstract words, more generalized words, are models of those models. Some call them Meta words. They streamline things by deleting the behavioral or observable data. The trade-off is that we gain the ability to condense or streamline our speech, but the loss is in specificity of observable behavior and meaning.

The Process of Elimination in Establishing a Desired State

Often, environmental changes were attempted by clients in futile attempts to stop the negative kinesthetic response to the varied stimuli that triggered each of the individuals. Examples of what clients change in their attempts are lovers, careers, loyalty to a professional school of thought, jobs, automobiles, residence, business partners, religion, lifestyle, and more. Often the process of the change is subjectively and vaguely perceived as a process of elimination. That is, the limitation is a known phenomenon. And as lists of personal objectives are formulated those choices which would elicit the negative kinesthetic are eliminated. Goals are de-escalated until they drop beneath the threshold of subjective discomfort.

Typically, the client choice dilemma is either to select "successful" objectives with intensely negative kinesthetic responses or to select "unsuccessful" personal goals which are not satisfying, but at least are emotionally tolerable. As one individual stated the issue: "I'd rather be chronically frustrated and a failure than chronically scared out of my wits." That mental set established the repetition of the pattern since the "leftover" goals they could handle were not based in choice, but in compulsion.

Analogously, in an episode of the TV serial *Buffalo Bill,* Bill, the fictional talk show host, makes passes in turn at each female on the TV set and is rejected one by one. He then proceeds, in desperation to avoid a lonely evening, to proposition less and less desirable individuals. Finally, the janitor is perceived as less painful than a lonesome evening even though the janitor meets none of his criteria of desirable companionship. The janitor is all that is left once other options are eliminated.

The deceptive feature I discovered in eliciting a desired state is this: The client image of a desired state is contaminated by their inability to even imagine the well-formed outcome. It is like asking a six-year-old to imagine great sex. It is not in their experience.

You will likely have to help the client construct a well-formed outcome. To do so you might use a behavior generator, a filmstrip, submodalities or possibly reframes.

The Competitive Reframe as an 80/20 Intervention

A useful "fix" for one form of conflict is Yeager's Competitive Reframe. I first mentioned this in about 1979. I found a number of cases that shared the common denominator of dominance or pecking order characteristics as the main issue. The item was a major issue in these cases, although not the primary issue at stake.

The demands of life require people to be assertive and competitive, yet all of these cases were stopped from this normal "looking out for No. 1" response by its having been distorted into a "good/bad" or possibly an "either/or" subjective definition. This hardening of the categories presupposed there was no middle ground for the sufferers where they might be occasionally assertive on the issues at hand. A reframe of their competitive response was in order since it was also tied up in conflict.

In their model a person "behaved" or else felt anxious, depressed, helpless, confused, or some other related negative response. It is notable that their careers had little or no progress in terms of upward mobility or financial success. It is notable that lack of success in accumulating money was a cultural fad in the 1960s. Now the tide has turned and financial gain and material success is being sought by many of the middle-aged former flower children. "Abundance consciousness" is the new euphemism for materialistic goals.

This leads to a distinction I make between a Disney-like, "nice-guy" world view and a law-of-the-jungle "survival" world view. Many people are in a competitive, hierarchically-dominated organization-man type of competitive experience day to day. Yet they delete that information from an assessment of their situation and alternatives. The result is usually a "blame frame" attitude toward events that are not "fair." This translates into disappointed dependency on others to provide goals that the individual ought to be able to provide for himself or herself.

In this context we will find this an exceptionally common "either/or" pattern—that of cooperative vs. competitive behavior. The demands of life call for flexible use of both ends of this particular continuum. Yet, in each case referenced here, the individuals were stopped from appropriate "looking out for No. 1" competitive responses. By having learned inhibiting definitions of their options, these individuals could not be effectively assertive or competitive in the context of achieving these items: a) financial gain b) upward mobility and c) interpersonal assertiveness.

These were three specific content areas where conflict coexisted simultaneously to inhibit goal achievement. These are the result of Modal Operator or Cause and Effect types of Meta model violations.

Competitive reframes work well in this event. The common denominator I got curious about in all of these cases was a conflict between what was wanted consciously vs. what was "allowed" to be achieved according to prior conditioning that operated subliminally.

There was no perceived middle ground for these individuals when they might occasionally use behaviors selected from the full spectrum of the implicit continuum of alternative behaviors. Either the individual "behaved" in accordance with the given category or else the person experienced intense negative feelings of anxiety, depression, guilt, helplessness, confusion, or some other negative kinesthetic.

"Wrong Category"

A common mental process associated with nominalizations is something I call "wrong category." The most typical example I find is when a natural event occurs as a continuum, but the client perceives the event as either/or in nature. In statistics, it is the distinction between "discrete" vs. "continuous" phenomena. Gender is either male or female—clearly an either/or category (Renee Richards notwithstanding). Height is a continuous item with an infinite number of gradations between, say five feet tall and six feet tall. We just conveniently scale the continuum in inches or fractions of inches as suits our purpose.

People who perceive events in the "wrong category" limit

their behavioral potential by their lack of access to options. The "wrong" use of either/or is exemplified by the phobic who is either in a phobic state about, say, dogs or is not in the phobic state. A continuum of phobic to anxious to cautious to affectionate to joyful response to dogs is more useful. It works in reverse, too, if one wanders about in the "grey areas" and can't make up one's mind to decide or not to make a given either/or choice such as whether or not to go for a goal. Either one does or one doesn't.

Nested Time Cycles

Another aspect to the strategy of modeling and labeling the function of behavior is time. The timing of the cycle varied, but in all these cases the timing was "nested." The TOTE of the fourtuple was stable, but operated simultaneously at two, three, or four levels of response and timing. A Tote is a conceptual model of the boundaries of a unit of behavior. For example, chronic lateness to engagements was a daily symptom. At the same time, weekly or monthly aversions would occur such as avoiding unpleasant staff meetings or school classes.

Also simultaneously operating might be an annual or bi-annual change of jobs or lovers as the given anchor was triggered by events. Thus there were sets, sub-sets and sub-sub-sets of information that matched my mental template. As is colloquially stated, there were wheels within wheels within wheels. Thus, fixing a leveraged and generalized fourtuple is likely to "clean a client's clock," as it were, in an application of the 80/20 rule.

On occasion, it takes a bit of figuring to identify the client's substantive issues in contrast to their limited understanding of their limitations. Clients, such as those mentioned above, presented statements such as, "I want to be successful, to make something of my career." This conscious goal was followed by a list of "I can't" reasons citing skill limitations (how to) or situational limitations (chance to) that stopped them from getting results.

The unconscious pattern, as revealed in incongruities of expression, disclosed that the "I can't" reasons were emerging from the unconscious.

The feelings they experienced were available to the conscious self mostly in the form of bad or unpleasant feelings (negative kinesthetics) associated with the presenting problem of an unachievable desired state. They did not have access to alternative modes of resolving the conflict through their own programming.

We might colloquially refer to this as a lack of "willpower." In examining the conscious vs. the unconscious issues, the statements that indicated Meta model violations often took this form:

Conscious: I want to express my feelings (i.e., not be shy).

Unconscious: Nice children are seen and not heard (except in very limited contexts like reciting in class).

In a nutshell, the unconscious program had been installed and presumably the anchors that ran it had been "stacked" by years of experience. The unconscious program that limited behavior to one pattern effectively opposed the conscious desire. Such a program also eludes the average person's ability to change it unilaterally without another person's help. The intervention usually was oriented around the idea of expanding the ability to make choices for alternative behaviors that would allow routine day-to-day choices that matched the intentions or desires of the individual.

Syllogisms as a Model

Limiting patterns of this type are the mind's way of developing the psychological equivalent of syllogistic logic that is found in college philosophy courses. Syllogisms are a philosopher's tool for expressing relationships among logical possibilities of ideas. For instance: If "A" = "B" and "B" = "C" then "C" = "A." Such syllogisms are the rough equivalent of the rules of a sports event (football) or a board game (Monopoly). A definition of the topic is established, a set of rules for how the game is played is defined, and criteria for internal consistency, "scoring" and "winning" (i.e., a well-formed outcome) are also defined.

In games, the people involved know it is a game and can choose to walk away from it. They are able to "outframe" the game and its requirements simply by ceasing to play. However, we seem to need a little extra help in lots of situations to be able to outframe our own internal limitations.

The practitioner's practical problem with syllogistic logic (the equivalent of Meta model violations) is that such logic is a closed system and does not admit ideas that are outside the original frame of the definition. I like to "outframe" the syllogism by expanding the client's mental parameters with techniques like reframing and submodalities.

This "either/or" pattern then follows this way: Either I am inexpressive and shy (the payoff is to be approved, but also goal-frustrated—which has a bad feeling) or I am expressive and heard (the payoff is to be disapproved and goal successful which also has a bad feeling). A typical case is the person whose success makes them feel guilty. The preferable option of being expressive and approved (with a positive feeling) has been rendered inaccessible and therefore deleted from the individual's response potential.

The practitioner then would appropriately search for the occurrence of an historical client psychological event to serve as a resource anchor. Of course, the anchor would need to combine "expressive" and a positive feeling. The practitioner would then stack the positive anchor and install the pattern as a behavioral option.

This also is a model of how double binding works for some clients in that we are virtually *all* criticism phobic and yet the source of approval and criticism is usually from the same place . . . an authority figure (i.e., a parent or other persons with similar characteristics such as a boss). Richard Bandler calls this conflict pattern "Go away . . . closer."

Selecting Interventions

The frame selected for handling the pattern in these cases was to define and tentatively label the leveraged issue as a conflict. Of course, there were other ways to define the issues, but I tested the notion of the cases as subliminal conflicts. When defined as such, a conflict (or whatever label is at issue) lends itself to a variety of interventions.

For instance, as an intervention one might use a six-step reframe on the part that protects the person from the negative feeling; a three-step dissociation from the negative feeling (contextualized in relevant ways, of course. We wouldn't want them to feel good about rape, robbery, etc.) We could also use a submodality procedure that changes the negatively charged kinesthetic images to match the positive images and anchors elicited.

It might have been just as easy to have "defined" the problems as phobic responses to success. But I would not be entirely optimistic that the definition would have covered as many bases as elegantly. The choice of label is based in observation of fourtuples and by matching them to the best fitting model you have in your repertoire.

In any event, the intervention technique selected is focused on the motivation of the person. The obvious reason: what a person wants is the basis of their ecological balance. Also, what a person wants serves as their organizing principle for their attention and efforts. If someone wants something intensely they will learn how to do it or else select situations where they have a real chance to succeed at their goals. It was not, in these cases, a *how to* problem. It was a *want to* conflict disguised as the "fault" of the situations *(chance to)* the person was in.

This pattern is common. Of course, there were varying degrees of conscious awareness of the mechanisms and compulsivity involved. The outcome, of course, is to install additional behavioral potential by adding positive response choices at the trigger point of the behavior. Pervasive, positive changes are the desired result. Of course a gaggle of other techniques might be used as additional issues emerge calling for interventions such as behavior generators, filmstrips and synthetic referential indices.

Yet, for all of the characteristics a label may have, the label becomes the medium of the power of the practitioner.

CHAPTER THIRTEEN

ON BUILDING ELEGANT CHAINS IN METAPHORS

Imagine yourself as the client listening to your practitioner telling a metaphor that is irresistibly relevant to your situation. You are absorbed in a light trance state as you generate interior images to match the story line. The scene is reminiscent of the golden days of radio when imagination reigned over the prefabricated images of television. You are involved in the story.

The speaker has your mind moving toward the conclusion that will affect your life, your feelings, your choices about your future. And suddenly the storyteller jars you out of your experience. You have been startled out of trance into a state best described by "Huh?! What happened?" What *faux pas* has the practitioner committed?

Possibly the storyteller has accidentally shifted from the artful imaginary vagueness of Milton model to the very concrete terms of the Meta model. Maybe in transitioning the referential index from the story's main character (e.g. "he" or "she") to "you," the handling was clumsy enough for you to notice. Maybe the shift of scene from general to specific was too abrupt. In any case the experience is a form of the proverbial "rude awakening." Your practitioner must regain the mood and carry on. No real harm is done but it is a needless distraction.

The basics of pacing and leading are taken for granted with an experienced practitioner of the subtle arts of Neuro Linguistic Programming. But when a story doesn't flow smoothly for the client, the culprit is most likely to be found in the absence of elegance in producing smooth transitions from one element of a metaphor to the next. Smooth transitions are the glue that keep the "chaining" procedure and the story elements together.

To lead the client's imaging from beginning to end of a story calls for a series of story elements to be chained together. Those links must be "logical" in their sequence, chunk level, and especially in their "connectedness" to one another. Transitions make the connections seem natural.

A story may shift back and forth in time. The client may think the story will end and you flash back to an earlier scene and the client goes with you—possibly pleased that the story hasn't ended and that there is more to come. Possibly you have built in some loose end that the client has forgotten and you gracefully pick up the thread and lead him or her in entirely new directions. For example, "As the transformed caterpillar started to shed her cocoon and spread her beautiful wings she thought back to the times when she wanted to believe 'I can do it now. . . .'

A nice easy transition of this type lets you delay the final transformation with a flashback as you help the client finish up any unresolved items of concern. By comparison, how does this seem? "As the transformed caterpillar started to shed her cocoon she thought about all the problems she'd had and wanted to be sure if she was ready to fly . . ."

Now if you can't sense the difference in these two transitions to a flashback you ought to give yourself a mild depression as punishment. The difference is: elegance. The first is positive in its presuppositions and gives a nice chance to embed the command, "I can do it now" while the past is nested positively in the present moment and presupposes she always wanted to change.

The second example risks eliciting the original negative state and raises doubts about her ability to fly now, which would pretty much neutralize any embedded command about "ready to fly" which is also not as generically suggestive as "I can do it now . . ." since "it" is left to the client's imagination to attach meaning. "Fly" must be translated from literal to metaphoric meaning and adds an unnecessary step to the imaging process. "Fine points!" you say? Maybe. Try it both ways. Odds are you'll like the results of the first approach better.

A practitioner must be able to create those kinds of dynamics, and a good metaphor will handily manipulate the listener by manipulating the action, moving back and forth through time, from scene to scene, from character to character. It gives the audience (of one or many) the pieces of a puzzle with flexible parts that imagination (and transderivational search) forms to fit their individual needs. The audience is captivated and enthralled.

Good storytelling is many things: Milton model, Meta model, synesthesia, anchoring, pacing, leading and more. Good storytelling is lightyears away from grade school stories such as "What I did at summer camp." Odds are that you told those stories in a chronological listing of events very much paralleling their actual sequence.

Of course the meaning of those events was not in their chronology but in their relevance to the makeup of your personality. Maybe you made your first real friend, or discovered sex, or became hooked on the outdoors. In the telling, though, you probably started with leaving home and ended with returning home.

You didn't know then about, say, flashbacks such as starting with the trip home and how you reminisced about your long-dead fears of meeting a busload of strangers. That calls for a different kind of skill—a flexibility that not everyone has learned. Yet the skill represents the kind of flexibility an accomplished practitioner should have.

The point is not that you should use flashbacks. That is only one metaphor technique. The point is that a metaphor is a series of anchors—a chain—and the elements of the chaining procedure must link to one another in ways that are congruent with imaging and perceptual mechanisms in general and with your client's needs in particular.

As a storyteller you can start a metaphor anywhere and jump backward (regression) and forward (future pacing) through a lifetime of the client's experience. You can bypass the external factors of time and regress clients to earlier realities. You can nest and merge elements of action, time, character and place. In bypassing the elementary framework of chronology, the storyteller can attend to client meaning and call the shots about when the client experiences what.

This shifting of components is heavily dependent on transitions. Transitions are the connective phrases with psychological logic built into them that get you through the maze of the client's needs. You can use the transitions to create elements that will put the client where and when as needed to make things work. One of a transition's roles is to oil the story machine. Another role of the transition is to link the elements of the metaphor into a cohesive whole.

Scan a few children's books and other sources of metaphors. You'll find they are conscientiously woven together to produce a trance-like effect. A transition that doesn't flow will change the client's attention from directed, internal reverie to a consciousness you are then obligated to return to a more receptive, less critical state.

When the story flows, you'll know it because the client won't notice . . . and that is what you want. The client can effortlessly follow your lead with imagination in full flower. When sentences and paragraphs lead into one another you know your story has an elegant flow.

"Flow" is one test of a good metaphor. How transitions are handled can make or break effectiveness. Transitions provide "psycho-logical" connections in the mind between story elements. A crude transition (or a missing transition) is like hitting a pothole in the road. In one breath your mind is in one place and in the next sentence you are someplace else and the sense of it is missing. Either you don't know why you are there or you are uselessly aware of the storyteller's lack of gracefulness.

Smooth transitions allow images to connect one to the other, building the chain from the present state to the desired state. A missing link such as a jarring transition is not much different than a kinesthetic chain which attempts to link disparate states. It doesn't work.

Smooth transitions get the audience from image to image without any awareness of how it happened because it feels logical—psycho-logical. If your story elements are just a bunch of ideas lumped one on top of the other, your outcome is going to resemble some form of hash rather than a smoothly sculpted thought pattern for your client.

A few examples will illustrate the point. "Meanwhile, her wings were beginning to emerge from the cocoon . . ." Sure. It brings you from one state (the past) into another (the present) in a very direct fashion. The device of "meanwhile" does pick up the action where it left off, and it is hardly an imaginative ploy. It can be jarring. The client can be suddenly aware of the external source (you) of the shift but you want the client to be aware of internal events.

If you have to get back to the transformation or any other aspect of the metaphor there are better ways to do it. Try this: "This wonderful new experience, she had thought, would lead her to the secret of change. And as she wished, she was changing at this very moment as one of her beautiful wings emerged to be gently fluttered by the breeze."

Suppose later in the metaphor you wanted to flash back to the transformation. Try this: "This puzzling encounter was very much what she had imagined as she emerged from her cocoon and began to satisfy her curiosity about the many things she wanted to experience . . ." And on you could go into arranging presuppositions, etc., that fit your story's theme.

The latter two versions provide an elegant connection between different chronological events. Transitions work as well when switching characters and places and any other elements you have built into the story. The well-worn "meanwhile . . ." is too elementary and can be a pothole, although congruent tones could help you get away with it. It is a natural type of conversational device, but it can dissociate the audience from the images and reverie you have endeavored to create. What you have undone you must recapture with renewed pacing and utilization to make it work.

What is a good transition? Logical, i.e., psycho-logical is the answer. As mentioned above, it keeps the audience associated with the story, it keeps the audience at least mildly entranced and it flows. Flow, in a sense, is a negative thing. When things flow you don't notice the seams in the story. This is actually rather natural. When we have rapport in conversations, we transition naturally: "Oh that reminds me . . ." is natural, but a bit jarring for a metaphor. And it is not likely to sustain a chain of images.

When the storyteller has an integrated set of skills, good transitions seem to happen naturally and without planning. Effective metaphors seem to have a life of their own. The best have a logical way of unfolding the story as well as unfolding the client's behavioral potential. A good story generates its own transitions almost without the teller having to consciously debate with how to do it. If you notice a "Yes, but" response in the audience, that is a good clue that you have lost their willing "suspension of disbelief." It's then time to tune up your transition-making strategy.

But an aside is required here. Experienced practitioners seldom start a metaphor by planning it in conscious detail beforehand. Preplanning an outline in detail creates the risk of boxing yourself into the plan and overriding the observations that tell you to spontaneously shift your elements as the client response dictates. Remember: Match the client's model —not yours. For the sake of practice just start your story and if you are ready, one sentence will logically lead to the next.

And remember, there are no mistakes in NLP—only outcomes.

What is a useful attitude to have about transitions? After all, they are only connective tissue and not the real muscle of the story. A transition can be a multi-faceted creature. It can be lots more than a sentence or a phrase that connects two ideas or thoughts together. It can end one line of thought and start another. "Now she could fly away and leave her past behind which, like her cocoon, had done its work."

A transition can steer the story in a new direction or indicate the passage of time. "As the season changed her curiosity grew . . ." or "Nature provided her with all the answers once she knew her way . . ." These transitions are leading devices that organize the client into logical overlapping images that transition smoothly from one to the other in an effective chaining process. Transitions allow you to blend elements as diverse as self, relationships, activity, goals, and many many more components of a story.

How else might we set up a transition? How about our old friend "but?" No, not the kind with two "ts." This kind: "But the change into a butterfly may change what you like to do from playing on leaves to floating on the wind." Or: "But if she thought being a caterpillar was fine, could she imagine being a glorious, soaring butterfly?" There are plenty of uses. You might go back through this article and decide if the last sentence in each paragraph relates well to the first sentence of the following paragraph.

As in all aspects of NLP, transitions are less about what you are saying than how you say it. Practitioners vary in storytelling skills. And effective transitions are a hallmark of the best storytellers.

An old radio show once ended an episode with the hero at the bottom of a snake-infested pit, totally surrounded by a tribe of hostile and hungry cannibals. "How is the hero going to get out of this?" the audience wondered. The next episode opened with the announcer intoning "After our hero got out of the pit . . ." A cheap trick. I still remember my agonized groan at the wreckage of my expectations.

A poor transition has much the same effect. Now go tell a story and have some fun.

CHAPTER FOURTEEN

TRUTH OR FACTION

You are wondering if there was a typo. But, no, I really meant "faction." There is a close relationship between fiction and faction. For example, in the world of professional writing and authoring, one form of the craft, faction, involves writing about real historical events with reconstructed information. The mixture of fact and fiction is known as "faction."

It doesn't pretend to be the literal truth, it is not fiction, yet it does represent the essence of the actual truth to be told. It is different than fact or fiction because it is designed to produce a different effect. Let's define it according to our deviant version of *Webster's Dictionary.*

Faction: not a political splinter group. The judicious mixture of fact and fiction to produce faction. Commonly known as a "white lie," it is a type of technique that effectively leads the client to a well-formed outcome or desired state vs. what would be possible with the literal matching of "truth" to the client's present state. Especially used in metaphors and reframing techniques.

Indications for use are when literal truth would not produce an ecological client result. Usually it refers to an embellishment or trimming of the literal facts to produce a given client response. Abraham Lincoln used faction in his stories virtually every day. Modern politicians are especially well-versed in it as is the news media.

A professional will have many occasions to tell faction to

clients when the effect is what the client wants and needs. However, we should not overlook the value of what the average married person has to teach us on the subject of faction. Certainly we could gather many specimens of excuses that would qualify as faction from the everyday experience of typical men and women. How did you explain to your spouse that the timing of your business trip to Rio inconveniently coincided with the arrival date of your mother-in-law for her two-week annual visit?

Naturally, I would not like to imply that only nefarious motives are to be associated with the use of faction. There are equally common uses of faction that have demonstrably positive motives. From a fair-minded, impartial survey of the faction's phenomena, let's take the sterling example of the Tooth Fairy. Any Philadelphia lawyer, possessed of his senses, would quickly concede that the operations of the Tooth Fairy involve a real tooth and real money. Only then would the minions of the law take us to task as to whether the exchange involved a genuine Fairy or the bald deception of a misguided parent, bent on deluding a hapless child.

Legal cynicism notwithstanding, this case clearly falls under the leniency clause of none other than the original Claus . . . Santa Claus. Is Santa merely another case of deception, I might ask! So! Are we also to accuse the Easter Bunny?! Would you tell a child the literal truth for its own sake or would you humor his fantasy? And besides, many feel that adults are simply large children.

I grant you. There are cases of abuse. The *National Inquirer* has been cast as the "faction center" of the nation. But many consider the *Inquirer* as entertainment and thus it is not a clear case of faction but leans a bit toward fiction and confuses the boundaries of our discussion.

Perhaps *In Cold Blood* by Truman Capote is a good example of faction. But plain lies are another case entirely. This is simply because I have to admit the Jesuits and Southern Baptists are persuasive on the issue of lies as being outside the acceptable limits of faction. However, I have heard convincing arguments for Pinocchio. The *New York Times* was inadvertently omitted from the survey on the ratio of fact to faction in the news.

But really. How are we to measure the occurrence and effects of faction in the news and other important media such as myth and soap operas? The news is probably the toughest case of sorting one from the other. Still: Are TV newscasters really as flippantly happy as they are in fact portrayed? Only Polyanna would buy it, I think. Faction is also a lot like TV wrestling. There is lots of beefcake (or bull if you prefer) being thrown around. So how come no one ever gets hurt? I leave the answer to the reader to decide: deception or faction?

The telling of faction has many aspects. For example, clients often need rationales and reasons for what you are doing in their behalf. However, the reasons you give them do not have to be literally true if they are psychologically true. A really good novel or movie is not literally true. Follow your spouse on a shopping trip or to a baseball game (depending on gender) and you will find out how tiresome factual life can be. That's why stories are different than actual reality. But if a fictional or even a factional story were not psychologically true, the audience would be lost and the story teller would be talking to him or her self.

Another aspect of the use of faction is often a function of how much the client needs to be aware as opposed to, say, the professional's need to be deliberately confusing about what is going on. For example, many clients use the desire to be "aware" as a way to avoid what they anticipate might be a painful session. At times, keeping such a client confused about certain items is useful.

Since we all know that NLP is as painless as a vanilla milkshake, responding to the client demand for awareness in a literal way would merely help sustain their "stuck" state. A bit of fluff that distracts them from that fruitless mode is likely to emerge from your lips as some mild form of indirection that would likely qualify as faction. For instance, you might decide to tell them a related metaphor from your own experience that is "embellished" a bit beyond the literal truth of what actually happened.

As you know, any professional storyteller has to keep the effects of the tale in mind or lose the audience. After all, deletion, distortion and generalization are all normal perceptual filters and I am only suggesting that you use them to good effect . . . not that you give your client a snowjob. In this aspect of your work, telling creative distortions is a good thing. Besides, one of our primary rules is to frame things positively. If the literal facts are pretty grim, we want to elicit a positive state to displace the unpleasant state. Being literal won't do them any favors.

Another item to consider is that we select our storytelling angle anyway by choosing what we notice and don't notice. For instance, a story can be told from the subjective frame of reference or from a dissociated or demographic frame of reference. That is, you can communicate information from a macro or micro perspective. In either case, the information is authentic.

In business coaching, a client will often have trouble understanding the relationships with superiors if their model of relationships is based on the subjective frame of reference of a family model as opposed to an abstract organizational frame of reference. In the organization, unlike the family, the individual is a cog in a larger machine which can be indifferent to the fate of any given individual. The field of literature gives an example that illustrates the point nicely.

A fellow named Tom Wicker wrote a civil war novel, *Unto This Hour,* which takes place during the Second Battle of Bull Run. It is a novel of wide scope with a large cast of characters, and the ebb and flow of the battle is presented in vivid detail. Not only is it presented from the macroscopic perspective, he also writes a lot of "faction" into it. He creates scenes that include historically documented statements and dialog of the real-life characters like Grant and Lee. He is reconstructing events to represent the truth of the dialogs, but does not claim that the word-for-word truth is reconstructed-only the essence of it to make the point at issue.

In contrast, we can consider the Stephen Crane classic, *The Red Badge of Courage.* Every high school graduate has probably written an essay on it. It is different from Wicker's novel in that it takes the perspective of the subjective experience of one soldier rather than the extravaganza of a panoramic view with a "cast of thousands."

In NLP terms, Wicker's novel is written at a large chunk level and Crane's is written from the small chunk level of the individual. In Crane's version of reality, the hero has about as much perspective on the battle as does an aunt walking across an oil painting while Wicker has lots of perspective and little feeling for the individual. Both approaches are effective representations of reality.

Neither is better than the other; both are fictional and both are true in their presentation of human experience. So we know that in telling "faction," chunk level is one of the aspects to consider.

Another way to utilize "faction" is through the contrast of Milton model and Meta model. I tend to think of Milton model as the technique of being artfully vague and Meta model the means of being artfully precise. For example, the Rorschach Inkblot test is a classic use of the Milton model in psychological assessment circles. The person sees in the blots what is consistent with their perceptual patterns.

Meta Model is the opposite in that it steers the client in precise ways to think a particular thought or image which is often like trying to nail jelly to a tree. A Milton-like statement would be: "You are feeling some things, I notice." Of course you decide what "things" I mean: you fill in the blanks for yourself. As for Meta model, how about this? "I wonder if you are aware of your toes?" I have given you a very specific thought in this case.

Faction works well in either case, but the edge goes to Milton model from the point of view that it lets the client construct their own truth. But that subjective truth is often going to be a client-constructed case of autobiographical faction anyway. We construct remembered reality in terms of current needs. So there is a bit of faction involved in the memory process itself. If you have ever loaned someone a lot of money, you know how they recall the conditions of the loan in a not-so-literal way. That is a true case of faction-a little fact and a little fiction, i.e., faction.

The essence of the issue at stake here is very simple: what is the right way to "chunk and tell?" The answer is also simple: In whatever way matches the model of the client. In order to utilize what is going on you need to match the model of the client and you also need to "utilize" the information presented by the client.

When you match the client's reality, are you better off telling fact, fiction or faction? It pretty much depends on the client. If the client's whole approach to reality is to construct personal fiction that has no correspondence to anyone else's reality, then they are telling personal fiction. We all know how boring it gets to listen to the exaggerated bowling scores of even our best friend. It is rather like being exposed to home movies. There is nothing wrong with it. But the average person wishes that they could vanish along with cigar smoke into thin air.

Why bother to match the client reality at all if it is a limiting reality? Well, it is rather like using the right fork at a White House reception. It doesn't get the food to your mouth any better but it makes all the other folks more comfortable than if you don't. Fingers are more natural eating implements, but few of us would insist that eating "au naturel" is therefore preferred. We'd match their preferences, and client issues work the same way.

In the case of our two novels, each author provided just the right amount and level of detail to tell the story convincingly.

A wealth of technical detail enriches the macro-oriented book of Wicker. Without a realistic background it would not work any more than a Western movie set in the 1850s would make any sense with an Oldsmobile parked alongside the horses at the hitching post.

But Crane's book is not a story about abstract models. It is focused entirely upon the courage and fear of one soldier and can take liberties with the setting. Lots of contextual detail would have weakened the story. As you decide how you are going to tell your stories, reframes and metaphors to your client, it makes a bit of sense to figure out how your own experience will be factored into the situation. If you are a janitor or a general, you have many common experiences that are universal to others.

Otherwise, how would it be possible for the characters featured in television situation comedies to have such a mythic impact on American mores? Everyone's experience provides a basis for metaphors . . . even if they are the case of the horrible example of what not to do. The question then becomes: "How much truth to tell?" The answer is; "Whatever will match your client's model. And that may range from their preferred representation system and preferred accessing cues to their models and subjective referential indicates.

On the other hand, it is possible to overdo your own references to subjects that are obscure to the client's frame of reference. For instance, it is possible that some people will read *Moby Dick* for a lesson in the anatomy of whales, but most would be curious about the meaning of Ahab's quest. In essence, your selection of whether to focus on truth or faction or fiction depends on the way you want to lead your client from one state of mind to another.

If you have a feel for the nature of storytelling and you have an ability to read your client's behavioral cues, you will find the proper mix of fact, fiction and faction. But since you are guiding the client through the client's own territory, you will be making various choices along the way to the clients preferred Holy Grail. There are lots of reasons both pro and con to decide about which of the approaches (fact, fiction or faction) you will select at any given point.

Here are some of the reasons we may think of. We may be inclined to make up something factional because we have no real knowledge of a particular topic. Maybe we are lazy, or maybe we are impatient for results. Or perhaps we are not confident that our stories will be interesting to others. Maybe others of us are too literal out of some archaic fear that we must tell the exact literal truth or horrible, unnamed consequences will befall us. We may fear that some form of ignorance will be revealed about us. Or maybe we feel we don't have the right perspective, or that our personal experience can't match the client's. (If you think you have had troubles in your life, just talk to someone who has escaped the concentration camps of World War Two. You are bound to feel one-upped in the disaster department.)

Really good faction is relatively easy to do. Most of us have the rough equivalent of a master's degree in it. Faction means telling "make-believe" or "let's pretend" stories that have convincing clout in them. For instance, you may find it satisfying to tell of how you planned your trip to Rio in total innocence about its overlapping with the visit of an odious in-law. However, make sure you can keep a straight face as you recount the story in case there are any unsympathetic passers-by.

Of course, not everything that has happened to you will be easily formulated into attention-riveting stories of faction. Few of us can invent an "in-laws" story or even a *Star Wars* episode on demand which will sound like real fact.

Yet the *Star Wars* stories embody the age-old theme of good and evil that has always been with us. Few of us have met an in-law as purely evil or good as either Darth Vader or Luke Skywalker. But such themes continue to provide fodder for our factional efforts. If you can take such themes as intrinsic to know how we all think and feel, then the issue is a matter of how much faction you decide to factor into your mixture of fact and fiction.

CHAPTER FIFTEEN

RESEARCHERS GUIDE TO NLP

In the field of behavioral science, and behavior modification in particular, the stimulus-response model is the basic unit of observation and measurement. NLP uses the same model but at a new level of refinement.

Psychology Today magazine has commented on how NLP works: "What [NLP] accomplished was to reduce to formulas . . . how a person takes in sensory impressions, mentally organizes them in cognitive processes like memory and decision-making, and then translates the sequence into a response." ("People Who Read People," July 1979.)

To make the point in an unequivocal way: NLP is a science and a technology with a proven track record of results. This brief orientation is only meant to be suggestive of how NLP relates to behavior modification and cognitive psychology.

As a result of NLP's advances, severe emotional states such as anxiety, depression, phobias and compulsions are typically and lastingly modified to the client's satisfaction by NLP procedures within an hour. Cognitive performances such as spelling, reading, writing and math are equally as responsive to improvement with NLP technology. We might add that performance in leadership, advertising, sports, piloting aircraft, pistol marksmanship and other such endeavors yield equally well to NLP behavior modification procedures.

The intent of this discussion is to point out some similarities and differences between NLP and other approaches to behavior change. Behavior modification and cognitive psychology are the contrasting views which will be discussed here.

Since publication lag is partially the source of a serious gap between the discoveries of NLP and its fullest possible application to the behavioral sciences, one of the outcomes hoped for as a result of this discussion is to increase communications between NLP and the cognitive and behavioral schools of thought.

In the meantime, the main population to suffer is the consumer of psychological services who has only limited access to methods which produce rapid and cost-effective behavior change. Also, researchers anxious to achieve results will ultimately re-invent the wheels that NLP has already discovered.

Conditioning vs. Images within the "Black Box"

The S-R model tends to ignore the phenomena that occur in the mysterious "black box" of the mind. NLP has discovered that the phenomena of the mind between the S and the R can be observed, documented and manipulated experimentally with great precision. Cognitive psychology has come close to identifying these events, but is still at the trial-and-error stage. NLP is much more advanced than even the work of Beck at the University of Pennsylvania where NLP has been presented for discussion.

In an ordinary dialog where the S is a question and the R is an answer, there is a typical half-second to two-second lag time between the S and R. NLP has discovered that in the moment of time between the S and R there occurs a series of cognitive events that range from several to several dozen in number. These events are subjective memory images that occur in the mind and are representations of external events previously experienced and learned via the five senses.

That is, the subjective experience within the person's mind occurs in memory images that represent the five senses of sight, sound, touch, smell and taste. In other words, people neurologically reproduce experience in the form of mental images. Some of the imagery may be conscious although much of it will be unconscious.

Imaging has recently become a popular topic. However, the emphasis in mainstream behavioral science has been on very limited aspects of visual imagery. A recent issue of *Psychology Today* (May 1985, "Stalking the Mental Image," by Stephen M. Kosslyn) shows that the approach to imagery is piecemeal in issues such as finding parallels between human image management compared to computer image management.

There is no intent to identify practical applications or to integrate the findings with the ability to manage human behavioral concerns in areas such as business, therapy or education. This academic theme tends to be rather constant. However, there is now even a conference being offered as "The First World Conference on Imagery" in San Francisco sponsored by Marquette University.

Notation System

On the other hand, NLP has developed a notation system to chart the events of the cognitive processes for all five sensory image systems. Imaging events, (i.e., the cognitive events represented in the mind in the terms of the five senses) and their external behavioral manifestations are represented generically by this notational model: $[VAKOG]^{ie}$. The model represents the events that occur subjectively to the person and externally to the observer.

The events are represented by the sensory mode in which they are perceived and recorded in the brain. That is, V = visual, A = auditory, K = kinesthetic, O = olfactory, and G = gustatory. The superscripts represent: i = the internal imaging events and e = the externally observable effect of the internal imaging events.

Actual behaviors that are mapped with this notation system are as complex as anything found in physics or organic chemistry. Many examples are found in Dilts, et. al. (1980) and the idea is referenced in the glossary.

A very important difference between NLP and other approaches is the distinction between thinking and feeling. In NLP feeling (i.e., K for kinesthetic in the notation system) is defined as a cognitive event. That is, feelings are thoughts, too. As expressed colloquially, the experience of *intuition* is a kinesthetic mode of thinking.

Without going into detail on the nature of the images, suffice it to say that these images occur in complex series and combinations of cognitive processing events. Submodalities are discussed below in this connection.

Graphically, images can be represented in the following way.

$$S\text{------------------------------}R$$

Each dash in the line could represent a mental image. This is an oversimplified description of a thought pattern. The series of many events represented by the dashes can occur in less than a second or take many moments to occur. This represents what we all call thinking in everyday experience. NLP techniques are able to slow down and capture the image events between the S and R and observe them one by one.

From Dilts (1980) we have an illustration of what one person's learning fourtuple looks like as expressed with NLP notation.

Not all decision points, of course, are internal kinesthetic representations. Consider the following learning strategy:

$$K^e \longrightarrow V^e \begin{array}{c} \nearrow V^r \longrightarrow A^r \begin{array}{c} \nearrow K^e \longrightarrow K^i \longrightarrow EXIT \\ \searrow A^e \longrightarrow A^i_d \longrightarrow V^r \longrightarrow EXIT \end{array} \\ \searrow K^i \longrightarrow A^e \longrightarrow EXIT \end{array}$$

In this strategy, V^e and A^r are both decision points. The outcome of this strategy is for an individual to learn or incorporate some behavioral patterns. The person starts off by performing some physical movement or activity (K^e). Then, depending on what the external visual feedback (V^e) is for that action the person will choose between two subroutines. Within one of these subroutines, some remembered auditory experience will also serve as a decision point where one of two other substrategies will be selected.

Notice also that the V^r or A^e representations that appear at the end of two of the subroutines are also decision points that will either trigger an operation in which the strategy loops back on itself again, or moves on to exit.

This pattern could be used as a template and another person could be quickly taught this learning strategy, if desired. It is also worth noting that the teaching process could likely be achieved in an hour or two by using advanced NLP anchoring methods. However, the fact is that most if not all of this learning strategy is probably out of conscious awareness. Yet all of it can be made conscious. This is not necessarily an accepted "mainstream" fact.

As part of a current debate in psychological circles, consider this quote from the *Journal of Contemporary Psychology:* "In recent years, however, it has become commonplace to deny that we are consciously aware of the causes of our behavior." Daily NLP experience takes issue with that fashionable attitude. With standard NLP questioning techniques, it is entirely routine to elicit the unconscious causes of an individual's behavior and make the causes conscious and then to change those causes.

It is partly a matter of knowing *what* to observe, having quick methods of *"conditioning"* the person and *rules* of thumb (i.e., models) to guide one's choices of technique. Observing the behavior or thinking processes might include patterns of eye movements, word choice and patterns of word usage in addition to body language.

Anchoring vs. Conditioning

Anchoring is defined by Yeager (1983) as ". . . an exceptionally rapid means of establishing or utilizing a conditioned response using non-verbal or verbal language as the medium. The usual stimulus-response model of experimental psychology is *combined* and thought of as a single unit of behavior. The result is a more efficient means of working with behavioral phenomena." Yeager has also defined anchoring as the tool that produces "the intelligent reflex." Visually, this is how it looks:

$$S + R$$

Anchoring represents the discovery that internal, subjective mental events are subject to essentially the same laws of stimulus and response at this "micro" level of "imaging" behavior. Anchoring is a more precise measure of unique-to-the-individual internal events than is the more gross measure used in behavior modification at the traditional externally oriented S-R level of event.

NLP does have a fetish for observation every bit as intense as does behavioral psychology. But the coding system or mapping system is different, thus allowing intrapsychic events to be accessed by external observations.

That is, the S-R model and the Anchoring model operate in parallel at different levels of information. One of the differences, however, is that the S-R model is an external-only oriented rationale. On the other hand, Anchoring is simultaneously an internally and externally oriented rationale operating at a smaller level of detail in the information hierarchy of behavioral events.

NLP finds subjective, cognitive events to operate in very much the same manner that "reinforcement" operates at the customary level of observation typical of behavior modification. Three important characteristics of anchors are that a) they can be combined (paired) in ways that change the associated behavior; b) anchors can be strung together in long chains that change the associated behavior; and c) anchors can be used to modify particular images (simple or complex images) with submodality methods.

As a general rule, behavior is modified by changing the *Trigger* sensitivity to a stimulus, or by *Adding* behavioral units to a sequence, or by *Combining* units of behavior, or by *Separating* units of behavior. This is known as the TACS model and is expanded in the glossary.

An example of the differences between customary research and NLP is that the S-R behavior of "Anchoring" is dynamic in nature. Anchoring and images are discussed in other references. However, a brief list of characteristics can be illustrative:

Anchors can be merged (collapsed).

Anchors can streamline (speed up in response time).

Anchors operate in all five senses.

Anchors can operate singly or in extremely complex combinations.

Anchors can be connected to one another or separated as needed.

Anchors can occur in repeating patterns or in unprecedented patterns.

Anchors in one sensory mode can trigger anchors in other modes.

Anchors can be "captured" and reworked to generate new responses.

Anchors are the basis of one-trial learning, i.e., the reverse of the phobic experience.

Anchors are consistent until modified or evolved by experience.

Anchors are different from but overlap with the idea of fourtuples.

Anchors can be conceived in the same large scale as the as S-R or on small scale as the events in between the S and the R.

Anchors operate in nested hierarchies with relative impact on behavior.

Anchors operate on whole fourtuples, strategies, images or the parts such as the submodalities of images.

Etc.

S-R Conditioning vs. Anchoring

Using the concept of "anchoring," NLP is able to utilize what has been defined as the "Intelligent Reflex"© and the "Cognitive Reflex"© (© 1983 Joseph Yeager, Inc.). Although there are differences, anchoring is the rough equivalent of the S-R model conducted at the smaller level of detail involving subjective-cognitive events. An anchor is conceived as the two-faceted S-R model being combined into a single unit.

An example will illustrate the idea. Can you not think of a pink elephant? Unless you are newly arrived from Mars, your mind has no alternative but to conjure up the thought of a pink elephant. That is a case of stimulus and response. However, if I continue: "Is that pink elephant still there?" Of course the answer is "yes."

In NLP thinking, the stimulus and response are now a paired phenomenon. No matter how many times I mention the pink elephant, it is there . . . complete with whatever other images in your five senses that accompany it. The fact that your behavioral repertoire has been expanded to now include the S-R combination of my words and your image means that I can get you to replay that image in your mind whenever I use my anchoring word. However, this anchor is probably *not* generalized. That is, anytime anyone mentions elephants you are not likely to respond with the image generated here in this context in response to this dialog.

The fact that NLP does not assume the anchor would, or even should, generalize is a notable idea. Some anchors do and some do not generalize. The only way to be sure is to test it.

NLP has techniques to make it happen either way. It is a question of what suits the purposes of the practitioner at any given time. Everyone seems to respond to the S-R reinforcement principles at an external level. In contrast, on an internal level, the specific vocabulary of S-Rs is so unique, that the individual must be benchmarked for his or her own individual vocabulary of responses.

Fourtuples, Strategies and Differences in Scale

The serious researcher must learn some fundamentals about NLP before attempting to prove or disprove it. Otherwise the researcher only proves that NLP is not like anything that the researcher knows now. Of course it does not work like anything the researcher would know . . . NLP is an entirely different frame of reference.

A straightforward criticism of the typical research I have studied amounts to this: Too many researchers are studying NLP in blind ignorance. The results I have examined in the literature amount to the equivalent of a five-year-old studying adult sex and finding no value or meaning to it. Researchers need to do some homework before attempting to prove or disprove NLP's assertions. A good starting place is to read the references at the end of this article.

From a general frame of reference, the difference in scale between NLP and behavioral psychology is analogous to the difference between the level of the cell vs. the level of anatomy and physiology in biology. In mainstream behavioral psychology it is customary to ignore the internal "black box" events of the person.

NLP spends a great deal of effort on internal events that are analogous to the cellular level of biology. As a result of working at this more fundamental level there are important gains. One of the gains for applied situations is the routine use of "one-trial learning." That is, repeated stimuli and/or reinforcement schedules are not necessary to change behavior when the leverage of NLP rationales are used.

It only took one trial for you to learn to think of that pink elephant mentioned above. That elephant will be there a year from now if I ask for it. There are other differences in how the S-R model and the Anchor model are defined, but they are explained elsewhere (Dilts, et. al. 1980 and Yeager, 1983).

The "micro" cognitive events that occur during thinking have a recurring nature to them similar to computer programs. Each time a related stimulus occurs, the same internal response will repeat. In NLP the unit of behavior between the stimulus and response is called a "fourtuple" or a "strategy." The characteristics, components and processes of a fourtuple are too many to mention here, but the glossary will serve as an indicator of the many phenomena involved.

For the practitioner of NLP, observing and "anchoring" the elements of a fourtuple are the primary means of modifying behavior. An anchor acts as a tool to produce an appropriate conditioned response within the imaging system of the person's thought patterns. In general, the limiting and problematic behavior of a person can be modified by using anchoring to change a given image-element of a fourtuple. And it is also possible to engage or delete one or more additional fourtuples with the standard repertoire of NLP skills.

Adding Choices for Requisite Variety

Change efforts at a subjective, cognitive processing level expand the person's repertoire of accessible behavioral responses. In a broad sense, assisting the person to access additional behavioral potential is rather like teaching the person the language ability of expository writing. In that case, the person learns to use existing vocabulary in an infinite number of potential combinations to produce papers that match the task at hand.

The basic elements in memory (e.g., vocabulary, syntax, etc.) don't necessarily change but the ability to combine them in new configurations means new expressions of behavior are possible via the recombining of existing elements. This intervention work is where the notion of "programming" enters the NLP rationale. The mental process of manipulating data according to given "rules" (i.e., programs) determines the content of the result.

An important aspect of NLP logic relates to the idea of flexible (i.e., adaptable) behavior. In the study of systems behavior the Law of Requisite Variety takes an important place in thinking about why flexible behavior is a key aspect of success in achieving full potential. A system can be a person, a group of people, a computer, a car, a mind or any other phenomenon.

In the field of Ethology, for instance, it has been noticed that the animal with the greatest requisite variety is the most successful in adapting and surviving. The Law of Requisite Variety means this: In any system the component with the greatest number of behaviors will eventually dominate the system. In human terms this means that the person with the greatest available repertoire of responses is the person that will dominate that given system.

Limited behaviors mean that the person has less freedom of choice to produce the needed behavioral responses to manage the circumstances at issue. Social skills, academic skills, eating habits, and virtually any other item of behavior is successful to the degree that it operates on cue to produce the desired outcome.

A finding that is well-worn in folk psychology is that people are usually punished more than praised. This affects requisite variety in a powerful way. People are inadvertently conditioned to think more in terms of limits than in terms of possibilities of behavior. Negative frames of reference are so much more common than positive ones that negative programming dominates as a rule. This tends to make people get stuck in "I can't" logic, and they have the conditioning to make behavioral limits the rule instead of the exception. NLP changes this frame of reference to give the requisite variety to the developmental or "generative" type of behaviors.

The rationale of NLP focuses in particular on the ability of the technology to add behavioral options or behavioral potential to the repertoire of the person. The "choice point" for adding behavioral options occurs at the stimulus. Metaphorically at least, the stimulus is interpreted by the brain in a fashion similar to the decision-tree model found in data processing.

The learned response selected and engaged by the person is a function of the availability of various responses from the person's memory repertoire. An habitual response such as a "compulsion" means that the person has access only to a single and inappropriate response. At the choice point of the "S," NLP would install additional responses. Graphically, having a range of seven potential responses to a stimulus can be illustrated this way:

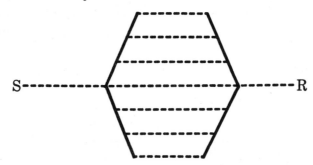

Theoretically, any number of relevant responses could be accessed from memory by the person. And each of the seven horizontal lines can represent a positive, negative or neutral kinesthetic experience. And it is also worth mentioning that any one of these alternative behaviors could be at least as complex as the learning strategy illustrated above. Providing access to multiple responses is a staple activity of an NLP practitioner.

NLP Presuppositions about Imaging

Some basic ideas about S-R imaging from an NLP practitioner's point of view can be condensed to the items below. Experience and experiments show that the following ideas are useful for achieving predictable behavior change.

1. The mind works on *images* that are experienced as thoughts and feelings. That is, the thoughts in the mind occur as visual images, sound images and feeling images. Most people are aware of these mental events. Please note this crucial item: Images are not artifacts of other mental phenomena. Images drive externally observed behavior as surely as the gears drive the hands of a watch. If you change the images in a fourtuple, you will change the fourtuple's causally connected behavior.

2. As a person thinks in those images, the thoughts leave recognizable "tracks" on his expressions similar to the way a hiker leaves tracks in the snow.

3. If the same stimulus is presented to a person it will produce the *same* internal thoughts in response and the *same* external expression of those thoughts. It is called Instant replay after the television technique used in sports.

4. If a situation repeats, such as making a decision to order lunch or to buy a car, the same decision-making thought will repeat. (There are several identified "master programs" that repeat frequently, i.e., learning, memory, motivation, decision-making, curiosity, creativity, and one or two more.)

5. If a person is asked a question such as "How did you decide to do "x?" he will think the thought that is his decision-making method each time he is asked.

6. Knowing that cognitive behavior repeats more than people notice gives one leverage. All one need to do is ask how the person thought about an issue in the past that is similar to the issue being discussed with him.

7. By combining this information with other techniques one is able to modify behavior very easily.

8. Imaging is not new. This *is* new: the fact that imaging has characteristics that are lawful and reproducible by scientific method and can be manipulated according to specific procedures. With the technology properly used, it is possible to produce an "instant" conditioned response. This is a rather dramatic positive reversal of the trauma/phobia experience where the person instantly learns fear. NLP has learned how to reverse the process in virtually the same "instant" amount of time.

Submodalities

An additional feature of working with the NLP version of the S-R model is this: If we assume that each of the "dashes" in the above illustration represents a particular mental image, we will find that images of the five sense have specific characteristics called "submodalities." That is, the mode of visual imaging has many characteristics such as color, motion, size, distance, brightness, etc. The auditory mode has its own characteristics such as tone, pitch, volume and so on. The kinesthetic mode has weight, texture, size, motion and more. Smell and taste have various characteristics, but for the most part they are not important sensory modes for behavior modification work. However, as research topics, they have interesting possibilities. A checklist for research purposes is available on request from the Eastern NLP Institute. Permission to use it in research can be granted.

Each of these "submodality" characteristics can be modified and in turn each change will modify the external expression of behavior that is causally connected to it. *Images drive behavior* in a way that is analogous to how the gears of a watch drive the hands on the face of it. Obviously the work on these multifaceted items can be complex.

Yet, categorically, the customary multivariate statistical approaches *will not work* with these data. The causal mechanisms are known to operate within the person. To search for statistical "main effect" models and inappropriately discard the cause and effect relationships to deal with the artifacts of the parametric statistical approach. This brings us to related issues of scoring and instrumentation.

Scoring and Instrumentation

One disadvantage of research undertaken so far by experimenters is that they do not have an adequate understanding of either the phenomena NLP manages nor do the customary parametric statistical techniques apply with any real value to the phenomena of subjective experience. One key reason is that NLP "scores" the individual's responses *ipsatively* rather than *normatively*. When changing a person's behavior, one changes the particular mechanisms of that particular person. NLP does not change behavior "on the average."

Nonparametric statistics are much more appropriate to NLP work even if the topic is research instead of a private practice. Another important aspect to consider is that NLP operates more or less constantly with Content Analysis methods such as those used by David McClelland in his studies of motivation.

Another important difference between NLP and conventional approaches is that the S-R model tries to generalize behavioral laws *across* populations of people and NLP tries to generalize behavioral laws *within* the individual person. Change occurs within the person, not on the average. Of course, the distinction is oversimplified, but it serves to establish an overall framework for further discussion.

Behaviorally anchored rating scales are common in many aspects of behavioral research. There are differences here as well. NLP presupposes that if a person is questioned about what is *wrong* the result is to reinforce the negative frame of reference that assists in maintaining the problematic behavior. The NLP approach is to question the person about what he or she wants as a desired outcome. Positively framed questioning has the effect of beginning the treatment *during* the diagnosis.

Scoring or scaling behaviors in this frame of reference can be compared to an NLP presupposition of the nature of positive rationales in causing behavior change. In many questionnaires, the questions are framed to emphasize what is "wrong" with the person rather than what the person wants. For instance, in the Beck Inventory a typical item is framed this way:

0. I do not feel sad.
1. I feel sad.
2. I am sad all the time and I can't snap out of it.
3. I am so sad or unhappy that I can't stand it.

The negative framework for eliciting states of mind tends to strongly reinforce the problems the person presents. For instance, "Can you not think of a pink elephant?" Or try this: "Can you forget the number 222?" This will tell you that if an idea is presented to your mind you must process it to even get rid of it.

When diagnosing a situation, NLP emphasizes that the focus be on the positive outcomes the person wants to achieve. Otherwise, the effort tends to amplify the problems in the very act of attempting to help. The fundamental issue in this regard is: "What is the treatment goal?" In a nutshell, it is not the absence of behavior "X;" it is the presence of behavior "Y."

Inappropriate Methods

Also, many ordinary experimental procedures are ill-suited to the study of subjective behavior. One study put the subjects into a chair and immobilized their heads. Then they wondered why the behavior didn't act "as advertised." The mode of study was rather inadvertently akin to restraining the wings of a bird and then proving that it would not fly.

In the case in point, a subject was put in a chair and then stimulated to do behaviors that required body language for their execution. When the behavior didn't occur as expected, NLP was found "not significant." (See W.B. Gumm, M.K. Walker, and H.D. Hay, "Neurolinguistics (sic) Programming: Method or Myth? in the *Journal of Counseling Psychology,* Vol 29, no. 3, 327–330, 1982 American Psychological Association.). There were so many inappropriate facets to this study that it could serve as a classic example of how not to study the subjective realm of the phenomena of NLP. However, that will have to be presented at another time.

Meta Issues

A recent issue of the *Journal of Contemporary Psychology* contains some interesting commentary illustrating how NLP relates to current issues in behavioral science.

Psychology has long sought scientific status. And physics became its model. In fact it is Newtonian physics that has become the paradigmatic science for psychologists. But although psychology adopted its methods, it has never achieved remotely comparable results. One consequence of psychology's extravagant but unrequited affair with physics is a debilitating physics envy.

This book raises the possibility that the paradigmatic science for psychology might be not physics but evolutionary biology. The contributors draw on ethology, sociobiology, and behavioral ecology to illuminate preoccupations in behavioristic psychology.

The discussion continues to illuminate other points of interest. That is:

One issue is ecological validity: the extent to which an experimental result is generalizable to the world outside the laboratory. Physicists have to idealize phenomena by removing irrelevant features to isolate their essential structure. Psychologists took their cue from physics and idealized behavioral phenomena. They created environments shorn of all extraneous features in which experimenters could maintain inventories of the stimuli impinging on organisms. Thus was born the Skinner box and the laboratory maze. But results gleaned from these severe environments seldom generalize either to the behavior of animals in their natural habitats or to the behavior of human beings in normal environments.

Today the search for legitimate methods of idealization is psychology's urgent task.

It is here that NLP fills the need to provide methods that work. One of the differences is that NLP factors the observer into the process of science and does not attempt to presuppose absolute objectivity. Official NLP publications are written in the first person because the person doing the writing is part of the process.

In other aspects, the methods of ethology are routinely used by serious NLP researchers. NLP is not bound by conventional disciplinary boundaries. It also uses tools from cybernetics, linguistics, computers, anthropology and math. In fact Richard Bandler (1985) has characterized NLP as meta-disciplinary. One of the curiosities of this frame of thinking is the example that Richard has demonstrated mathematics to be a behavioral science. He often calls NLP an attitude as well as a field of knowledge: In fact the attitude is the essence of scientific method, i.e., curiosity.

However, we now come to an analogy between NLP and the relativity of Albert Einstein. NLP is to behavior as Einstein is to physics. This means that the headlong pursuit of psychology to find absolute laws has lost sight of the fact that human behavior is relative. As Einstein put it to a train conductor:

"What time does Zurich arrive at this train?" Time and motion can be relative and so can behavior be relative. The article continues in this fashion to make an important point:

> A related conclusion concerns the difference between species regularities and scientific laws. Scientific laws hold for all times and places. But biological species are evolving systems whose properties are contingent on a particular environment at a particular time (pg. 106). (In NLP we say: "Everything we say is true . . . *except* when it isn't," as a way of expressing this conundrum.)

Conditions vs. Fourtuples

Another item worth mentioning is that NLP does not treat abstract *conditions* like depression. Labels like "depression" or "anxiety" are not things an observer can specify in sensory-observable terms. It is a name or a "nominalization" which invites fuzzy thinking and miscommunication among researchers. NLP treats, instead, a fourtuple which is an operating unit of behavior that is specific, observable and repeatable. A fourtuple would qualify as an *operational definition* in behavioral terms.

It is worth an aside to mention that a state of mind such as "depression" is *not* a pervasive experiential phenomenon for the sufferer. This means that a person is only depressed *some* of the time, not all of the time, in even the worst case. This is an important fact in NLP technology. This means that the person accesses "non-depressed" states routinely during daily experience. NLP uses this phenomenon to advantage. Contrasting states are elicited and installed with a rationale similar to reciprocal inhibition (Wolpe 19**). Anchoring enables the practitioner to elicit and install a competing state in mere moments.

In contrast, in one of Beck's books, *Cognitive Therapy and the Emotional Disorders* (1976), Beck references a client who was treated for depression. The case commentary illustrates an important difference between NLP logic and cognitive psychology logic. Beck notes that a client's symptoms, "negative thoughts," persisted ". . . until he recovered from his depression." Consider carefully what has been stated: the depression and the symptom of "negative thoughts" were conceived by Beck as different phenomena. Beck apparently treated the abstract idea of the "depression" instead of the specific behavior of negative thoughts. In contrast, NLP would treat the fourtuple of "negative thoughts."

The common error of assigning a *noun* to a process is one of the common errors found in typical language patterns that tend to distort reality. This *"thing-ifying"* of processes makes the researcher work on a false issue. There is no such thing as depression. Depression is an abstract idea and as an abstraction is not amenable to modification. NLP insists that all operations focus upon sensory-based observations because it is the mechanism of behavior that is the source of potential change. Any clinical goal in NLP must be stated in positives, be testable in the office or in the field, be within the person's control and be ecological to the person's own values.

In NLP logic we find that there are subjective behavioral states that are expressed as fourtuples. Fourtuples have their own mechanisms and characteristics. In their expressed form the fourtuples also have the ingredients of change built into them as the reciprocal. All one needs is the coding structure to notice and change them. This is typical of the different conceptual models between NLP and behavior mod and cognitive mod.

There are a dozen of these language patterns in addition to "nominalizations." They are found and explained in Bandler and Grinder (1975) and named "The Meta Model." The diagnostic questions derived from the Meta model are the reciprocal of the Meta model language pattern that limits a person's

cognitive functioning. The questions correspond to the reciprocal of the language pattern itself and elicit the unconscious
or subliminal process for observation and modification.

Thus the diagnosis of a person's limits has to do with the
actual expression of behavior . . . not with a theory that sepa-
rates the person from the observations. The person's cognitive
performance is always the focus of attention. The questioning
and diagnosis do not operate from a theory.

The questions come from the indicators that tell the practitioner exactly what to do. Of course this implies that we do
not ask, "How is this person similar to or different from other
depressives?" Rather NLP asks: "How does this person know
how to be depressed?" NLP considers the depression a learned
behavior and thus is a skill. The skill is usually being used
either in an inappropriate context or it is a signal from the
person's unconscious value system to change something in the
self or in the environment. Thus we might ask: "How did the
person learn to know when to employ the skill of depression
and what purpose does it serve in the ecology of that person
at a conscious or unconscious level?"

Summary

Dissatisfacation with the traditional and ineffective approach to behavior is echoed in another related context by
Neisser (1982) whose attitude is mentioned in the *American
Psychologist* (February 1985, pg. 179). Neisser ". . . registered
his dissatisfaction with the orthodox psychology of cognition,
and particularly the study of memory. To him, the field has
little to show for a hundred years of effort."

The fact that the discoveries of NLP were made by a math-
ematician/computer scientist and a linguist seems to have
elicited resistance from the mainstream behavioral science
community. More than ten years ago Richard Bandler pub-

lished the procedure for the five-minute phobia cure. The fact tht so few behavioral scientists have implemented it may be partly a function of the often-encountered "not invented here" syndrome.

However, this implementation lag seems to be based to some degree on the fact that interested researchers have had difficulty verifying the claims of NLP in various experiments. In examining the literature and in collating literally hundreds of conversations with behavioral scientists, I have found recurrent themes that seem to account for a great deal of the slow acceptance of NLP in its earliest stages of development. (Of course more current indications show that clinicians are adapting the techniques if not always the attitude of NLP.) Two important themes are:

    1.   different assumptions and beliefs
    2.   inappropriate experimental methods

A few items in each category are merely mentioned in order to suggest some of the issues involved.

    1.   One-trial *positive* learning is possible and is routine in NLP; behavior change can be very rapid; behavior change is natural and painless, the subjective person is the reference point, not norms or comparisons to others; NLP uses positive vs. pathological frames of reference; behavioral observations and indexing vs. nominalizations is the measure; mental images are assumed to cause behavior; unconscious behavior can be accessed merely by asking an appropriate question.

    2.   Content analysis is a basic technique; simultaneous and complex behavioral gestalts are studied rather than isolated behaviors; context is always taken into consideration as an aspect of behavior (vs. methods that operate rather like studying the meaning of Shakespeare by analyzing the punctuation out of context); ipsative scoring is taken for granted; anchoring and one-trial learning are routine tools to be used; behavior is more plastic than has been imagined; NLP uses a hierarchical data processing model of verbal and non-verbal language as well as predicates, sensory accessing cues, repeat-

ing behavior, and non-parametric statistics; generalizations are not made across populations, instead generalizations are examined within the context of the individual.

All of these differences are merely the tip of the iceberg in the many ways that NLP differs from other approaches to behavior. In reference to clients who are resistant to conventional therapies, one of the basic assumptions of NLP is important. "The meaning of the communication is the response it elicits." This means that a clinician's lack of progress with a client is an echo of the practitioner's behavior. As such it is more a comment about the practitioner's lack of skill than it is about the nature of the client's issues or behavior.

This puts the burden on the practitioner to take the responsibility of giving clients the most advanced state-of-the-art assistance available. Of course there are many issues that are not touched upon in this brief discussion. However, this presentation is offered as a point of reference for those practitioners and researchers who take full responsibility to offer their clients the best that is available. And in a survey of progress in the field, the casual observer would have to agree that NLP has discovered more of therapeutic value in the last ten years than the field of behavioral science has in the last hundred years. NLP is truly a major breakthrough.

References

Bandler, Richard and Grinder, John. (1975) *The Structure of Magic.* Vol. 1 & Vol. 2. Science and Behavior Books. Palo Alto, Calif.

Barnes-Gutteridge, William. (1985) *Evolution, Behaviorism and Physics Envy. The Journal of Contemporary Psychology.* Vol. 30, No. 2. pp. 105–106, Washington DC: American Psychological Association.

Beck, Aaron T. (1976) *Cognitive Therapy and the Emotional Disorders. New York:* International Universities Press.

——— and Beamesderfer, A.: *Assessment of Depression: The Depression Inventory.* In Pinchot, P. (Ed.): *Psychological Measurements in Psychophar-*

macology, Modern Problems in Pharmacopsychiatry, Vol. 7. Basel, Switzerland: Karger, 1974, pp. 151–169.

Chauvin, Remy and Muckensturm-Chauvin, B. (1980) *Behavioral Complexities.* New York. International Universities Press.

Dilts, Robert. Bandler, R. Grinder, J. DeLozier. (1980). *Neuro-Linguistic Programming: Vol. 1. The study of the structure of subjective experience.* Cupertino, Ca. Meta Publications.

Kosslyn, Stephen M. "Stalking the Mental Image." *Psychology Today.* (May 1985) Published by the American Psychological Assoc. Washington, DC.

Lorenz, Konrad Z. (1981). *The Foundations of Ethology.* New York. Simon and Schuster.

McClelland, David. (19**). *The Achieving Society.*****

Monitor, The. (May 1985) Published by the American Psychological Assoc. Washington, DC.

Neisser, U. (1982) *Memory Observed: Remembering in natural contexts.* San Francisco. Freeman.

Peele, Stanton. (1983) *The Science of Experience: a new direction for psychology.* Lexington, Mo: Lexington Books. in *Journal of Contemporary Psychology.* May 1984. Vol. 29, No. 5, pp. 398–399.

Sommer, Linda D. Universal Reframes. Eastern NLP Institute Seminar. Trenton State College. May 1984.

Staats, Arthur W. and Staats, Carolyn K. (1963) *Complex Human Behavior.* New York. Holt, Rinehart and Winston.

Yeager, Joseph. (1983) *A Collection of Articles on Management and NLP.* Fourth edition. Princeton. Eastern NLP Institute.

GLOSSARY

ACCESSING CUES: observable body language cues that indicate which of the five senses a person is using to think with. Examples are body posture, breathing patterns, gestures, voice tone, voice speed and eye movements.

ANCHORING: an exceptionally rapid means of establishing or using a conditioned response using non-verbal or verbal language as the medium. The usual stimulus-response model of experimental psychology is combined and thought of as a single unit of behavior. The result is a more efficient means of working with behavioral phenomena.

AUDITORY: refers to the sense of hearing.

BEHAVIORAL FLEXIBILITY: the opposite of habit. The idea can refer to the development of an entire range of responses to any given stimulus as opposed to having habitual, and therefore limiting, responses which would inhibit performance potential. Synonym: Behavioral repertoire.

BEHAVIORAL MODELING: a teaching technique in behavioral science for imitating the demonstration of a successful behavior. It has been superceded in effectiveness by the refinements of NLP technology.

BODY LANGUAGE: includes the popular notions of gestures, and other stylistic items of behavior that can be used to distinguish behavioral units. Also included are voice characteristics of tone, pitch, speed, pauses, accents, and other useful distinctions of value to the communicator.

CALIBRATION: the refined observation of body language expressions of internal states. Each individual will have a unique vocabulary of body language expressions. Defining their patterns is a powerful means of "getting to know" a person. Personal uniqueness must be defined initially in communications to insure successful dialogs.

CHUNKING: not the famous Chinese food. The concept of strata or hierarchies or levels of detail in observing and managing behavioral phenomena. The "chunk" level of generality, abstraction or detail is an important component in observing, assessing and selecting the type of intervention used to change behavior. Looking for a microscopic item of behavior with a telescope or vice versa is overcome. In classroom presentations, selection of chunk level is one of the important aspects of successful instruction. In coaching, interviewing, selling, counseling and other persuasive applications, use of appropriate chunk levels ensures the matching of an intervention to the behavioral item at issue.

COGNITIVE: refers to the mental processes of thinking and feeling. The idea is often distinguished from physical or "motor" skills.

CONGRUENCE: the absence of conflict in thoughts about a topic as expressed in words or body language. An incongruity example is when a person says YES to a request but subtly shakes the head NO.

FOURTUPLE: (4-tuple): a notational system for defining units of behavior used to map cognitive processes. Based on the five senses, all external and internal behavior can be expressed in combinations of (VAKOG), i.e., Visual, Auditory, Kinesthetic (feelings), Olfactory, and Gustatory. In most applications only V, A, and K are used.

FRIENDLY PERSUASION: The use of natural behavioral phenomena to help individuals make choices that achieve their goals.

FUTURE PACING: the mental rehearsal of a future situation that ensures the automatic triggering and use of a behavior learned in another context such as a classroom. Earlier literature referred to the issue as transfer of training.

GUSTATORY: refers to the sense of taste.

IMAGE: the mind operates directly from images that are received from the five senses. An individual thinks in sights, sounds, feelings, smells and tastes. See: FOURTUPLE for the definition of how images that represent memorized reality are stored and processed as thoughts which operate observable behavior.

INCONGRUITY: an external expression of an internal conflict. Often the individual will not be aware of the conflict between unconscious and conscious motives. A common example is the individual who promises a result that he or she unconsciously does not want to do. The outcome is typically reasons, alibis and excuses rather than results. The conflict can be observed in body language and verbal language.

INSTALLATION: the term for various techniques of installing behavioral changes. New behavior may be installed via combinations of anchoring, accessing cues or future pacing. This technological approach supercedes but is conceptually similar to behavioral modeling as found in the literature of behavioral science. See BEHAVIOR MODELING and FUTURE PACING.

KINESTHETIC: refers to the sense of touch or to feelings in everyday language. The concept incorporates all feelings of a tactile, visceral, motion, and emotional type.

LEADING: the variety of techniques used to lead the attention and thoughts of a person from one state of mind to another.

LOOPS (also looping): the inappropriate, usually compulsive repetition of a unit of behavior. In the literature also known as compulsions, obsessions and neurotic stupidity. Revived from computer terminology where a process has no accessible exit or termination point and thus recycles until stopped by external influences. Often the termination is a painful event inflicted by others in the form of criticism which displaces the pattern until triggered again.

In strategies (See Dilts, et. al, *NLP Vol. 1*) the procedure of choice is to install a subunit that designs an end point to the process after a selected number of iterations (e.g., installing a counting device) an amount of time, moments, days, etc., or other criteria such as external-to-the-person circumstances that end the pattern and lead to the next thought sequence.

MANIPULATION: the skill of messing up your own mind and goals by thinking selfishly in a win-lose mode instead of the win-win mode of mutual gain.

MEMORY: all stored experience in the mind exists in the form of images representing original sensory impressions. Memory images are utilized in the form of programs or sequences of images which directly operate behavior in the areas of thought and action.

META MODEL: A neurological and language-based map of cognitive behavior that identifies language patterns which can obscure meaning in communication. The Meta model provides a systematic means of questioning or probing to elicit the meaning needed to ensure successful communication.

METAPHOR: an alternative and directly parallel way of expressing one aspect of reality in the form of another aspect of reality. Examples are analogies and stories. The effect of using metaphors is to reorganize cognitive processes to enhance behavioral potential.

NEURO LINGUISTIC PROGRAMMING (NLP): the science and technology developed by Richard Bandler and John Grinder that surpasses the effectiveness of dynamic and behavioral psychology and can be classified as the state of the art in cognitive psychology. NLP expands its technological base rapidly and is the subject of many professional texts in applied areas such as education, management and psychotherapy. NLP is the first of the behavioral sciences to achieve technological breakthroughs in the aspects of human nature that are of everyday concern and provides the tools to change behavior previously thought inaccessible.

OLFACTORY: refers to the sense of smell.

OUTCOMES: the goals specified as the desired state of mind or performance. The NLP approach is to define outcomes that can be verified in sensory terms that are specific enough to generate a shared observation and agreement of their achievement.

PACING: the techniques of matching selected aspects of another person's behavior to achieve rapport. Effective pacing will produce a subliminal kinesthetic response of positive mood which provides the means for the content of a dialog to be exchanged with ease and effectiveness.

POLARITY: the mind compares sensory information to stored models or ideas of how reality has been previously experienced and organized. Upon receiving a sensory impression the mind matches the impression to the stored images. If the individual initially notices the aspects that match the image, this is called a positive responder. If the person notices the mismatch initially, this is called a negative or polarity response. (There is also the possibility of a neutral response if the stimulus has no kinesthetic value to the person.) Polarity responders tend to be called reactive, argumentative, or negative personalities if the predominant pattern is to initially notice what is wrong in comparison to their ideal images. These three patterns are learned and can be changed from any one of the three to another mode according to the desired effect.

PREDICATES: the image system a person is using is indicated by the word choice in the individual's spontaneous conversation. Words such as verbs, adverbs and adjectives are the items to notice and will correspond to the sensory image system such as: Visual- bright; Auditory- sounds like; Kinesthetic- feels good, etc.

PROGRAMS: patterned sequences of mental images that operate internal cognitive behaviors that in turn drive external behavior that can be observed. An important class of persuasive "master" programs are called strategies. Included are aspects of cognitive behavior with pervasive effects such as learning, curiosity, creativity, belief, reality, motivation, decision making and memory.

QOUQ: originally based on the Socratic method of managing dialogs to represent the strategy of question, observe, utilize, question. Developed by Yeager as a generic communication tool.

RAPPORT: the establishment of a cooperative communication mode where harmony, trust and positive emotional responses characterize the dialog. This is often achieved by pacing or matching aspects of the other person's (or persons') nonverbal body language which generates positive subliminal kinesthetic responses which enhance the communication.

RECURSIVE DESIGN: the use of the same principle or fact being taught to design the content of the teaching to be accomplished. This is a routine feature of NLP designs which greatly enhances its impact and value.

REFRAMING: a class of techniques for changing the meaning of a stimulus or event—usually from a negative meaning to a positive meaning. In an applied situation a negative reaction to, say, too high a price for an object can be reframed to being an indicator of its superior quality.

REPRESENTATIONAL SYSTEMS: a synonym for sensory image systems. Reality is stored in the central nervous system in the indirect form of neural images rather than the absurd notion of the skull being filled up with physical objects. Images "represent" physical reality.

REPRESENTATIONAL SYSTEM PRIMACY: the dominant sensory system or preferred image system that the person habitually uses. Personality characteristics and learning abilities are affected by a person being over-dependent on any one sensory image system. For instance, an auditory dominant person has limitations in being able to visualize items and vice versa. This can be changed to enhance the person's ability dramatically— witness the five-minute technique of training a poor phonetic speller into a successful visual speller with perfect recall.

SECONDARY GAIN: when a "problem" behavior actually has a positive payoff in some other frame of reference. A complaining "squeaky wheel" gets lots of attention, or a smoker gains relaxation from a "bad" habit.

STRATEGY: see **PROGRAMS.**

SUBLIMINAL: the behavior that operates out of conscious awareness. You didn't notice your toes in your shoes until it was mentioned now. This fact of selective perception has many uses to leverage the effects of performance-enhancing techniques. Examples are classroom design, placement of visual aids, use of gestures to engage neurological functions, or to condition responses to specific persons, locations, tones of voice, etc.

SYNESTHESIA: the combination of any two or more of the five sensory modes to operate interdependently rather than as a solitary sense mode. The gain is in enhanced cognitive power and flexibility.

TACS: the four classic modes of behavior-change intervention. TACS represents Triggers of behavioral units, Adding behavioral units, Combining behavioral units and Separating behavioral units.

TOTE: a mental model or rule of thumb used to map a generic sequence of behavior. The term represents Test-Operate-Test-Exit, which can be used as a behavioral boundary system to isolate and study units of behavior.

TRANSDERIVATIONAL SEARCH: the mental process of responding to a stimulus by searching through memory to find a reference experience from which to derive the meaning of the stimulus. It is an inward focus of attention as the person "thinks something over."

TRANSLATING: a technique of rephrasing words to elicit the other person's transition from thinking in one imaging system into another. If a person isn't "listening" you may be able to help them "see" your point.

UNCONSCIOUS: see **SUBLIMINAL.**

UTILIZATION: the opposite of being disappointed that an event is not occuring as expected or preferred. Utilization is being able to turn any event into good use. It is the ability to make a silk purse out of a sow's ear by selecting an appropriate technique to turn a situation around to one's liking. See **REFRAMING** as an example.

EASTERN NLP INSTITUTE™ TRAINING PROGRAMS

Our rapid expansion has allowed us to offer more programs and services than ever before. We want to thank our friends and clients for making the growth possible. In addition to the training programs described here, we continue to offer personalized assistance to individuals and, of course our consulting work to organizations has expanded.

The Institute is well known for its programs. Following are some applications and related program titles:

1. Certification Training: 10 month (commuter) & 15 day (residential) formats for Practitioner, through Trainer levels of skill. Taught by Bandler, Dean, Dilts, Drozdeck, Epstein, Levi, Sommer, Yeager and other superstar masters of NLP. All skills (e.g., strategies, hypnosis, advanced modeling) and all applications (e.g., therapy, business, education, medicine) are taught. Widely acclaimed as the BEST.

> **Princeton:** ten month program (one weekend per month) begins each October
> **Camp NLP:** 15 day (August residential) at an East coast location

2. CLIENT/THERAPEUTIC APPLICATIONS: ˙ Anxiety & Stress ˙ Phobias ˙ Relationships ˙ Divorce ˙ Depression ˙ Low Self-Confidence ˙ Learning and Career Disorders ˙ Weight & Eating Disorders ˙ Sex Therapy ˙ Insomnia ˙ Parent & Child Relationships ˙ Gambling ˙ Compulsions & Obsessions ˙ Hostility & Anger ˙ Boss & Subordinate Problems ˙ Social Inhibitions ˙ Assertiveness ˙ Drug Abuse ˙ Lifestage Crisis ˙ Lifestyle Enhancement . . . and more.

> **Choice Point:** two days with Linda Sommer; her famous Universal reframes will change you.
> **Belief Systems and Your Health:** Linda & Robert Dilts change your state of health - two days.
> **Hypnosis & Advanced Submodalities:** Bandler, Dilts & Sommer supercharge your skills.

3. ORGANIZATIONAL APPLICATIONS: Win-Win Communications ˙ Persuading Decision Makers ˙ Motivating Colleagues & Peers ˙ Ending Conflicts and Personality Clashes ˙ Coordinating Effective Meetings ˙ Influencing Programs & Policy ˙ Ensuring Administrative Follow Through ˙ Eliciting Hidden Agendas ˙ Handling Office Politics ˙ Overcoming Resistance to Change ˙ Clear Convincing Communications ˙ Changing Hardened Attitudes ˙ Coaching and Career Development ˙ Effective Performance Appraisals ˙ Selection & Assessment . . . and more.

> **The Psychology of Friendly Persuasion:** Selling skills for the professional salesperson.
> **New Applications of NLP:** The "A" Team brings you up to date on all the latest tools and uses of NLP plus recertification is awarded; Bandler, Dilts, Epstein, Sommer & Yeager.

4. PERSONAL GROWTH: Success is a function of how effective the individual is in delivering know-how to personal goals. Many of us feel limited in our ability to be 100% free of our self-imposed constraints. With NLP's innovative techniques, new ways of thinking, feeling and behaving are easily achieved by channeling your own internal resources to work for you to gain the personal efficiency and effectiveness to achieve your maximum potential.

> **Interpersonal Skills Lab:** Learn how to get along with anyone and achieve your outcomes.
> **Friends and Lovers:** A weekend for couples in the Bahamas; learn loving as an art form.

5. GRADUATE DEGREES are available in NLP (Accredited PhD & MS). Continuing Education credits are available.

Eastern NLP Institute PO BOX 697 Newtown, Pa 18940   215-860-0911

BOOK LIST
Meta Publications Inc
P.O. Box 565
Cupertino, CA. 95015

The Master Moves $14.95
Moshe Feldenkrais

Magic in Action $14.95
Richard Bandler

Roots of Neuro-Linguistic Programming $22.00
Robert Dilts (hardcover)

Applications of Neuro-Linguistic Programming $22.00
Robert Dilts (hardcover)

Meta-Cation: Prescriptions for Some Ailing Educational Processes .. $12.00
Sid Jacobson (hardcover)

Phoenix—Therapeutic Patterns of Milton H. Erickson $14.00
D. Gordon & M. Myers-Anderson (hardcover)

Neuro-Linguistic Programming $24.00
Dilts, Grinder, Bandler et al Limited Edition (hardcover)

The Elusive Obvious $20.00
Moshe Feldenkrais (deluxe edition)

Patterns of Hypnotic Techniaues of Milton H. Erickson, M.D. .... $ 8.95
Bandler and Grinder
Volume I (paper only)

Patterns of Hypnotic Techniques of Milton H. Erickson, M.D. $17.95
Bandler, DeLozier, Grinder
Volume II (hardcover)

Provocative Therapy $10.95
Farrelly & Brandsma (hardcover)

Gestalt Therapy and Beyond .... $ 9.95
Marcus (hardcover)

Changing With Families .... $ 9.95
Bandler, Grinder and Satir (hardcover)

The Structure of Magic, Volume 1 .... $ 8.95
Bandler and Grinder (paper)

The Structure of Magic, Volume II .... $ 8.95
Bandler and Grinder (paper)

Practical Magic $12.00
Stephen R. Lankton (hardcover)

Therapeutic Metaphors $10.95
David Gordon (hardcover)